Advance Praise for *Unbridled*

Launching into new phases in her life, including the pain and discomfort as well as the freedom and joy of the venture, Barbara McNally communicates what many of us suspect—to be truly ourselves we might have to journey in directions we hadn't imagined. Gaining confidence, finding passion and a life's mission along with lessons from her ancestry, McNally is an example for those of us invested in making our lives meaningful. Moreover, she writes a great story. You'll feel with her every step of the way.

—Sheila Bender, author of *A New Theology: Turning to Poetry in a Time of Grief*, www.writingitreal.com

What matters is not the destination, they tell us, but the journey. Whether the path we follow is a quest, a pilgrimage, or an exploration into memory, the ultimate journey can lead us into a deeper understanding of ourselves and our place in the world. Setting out on this odyssey requires courage, honesty, and a fair share of humility. In her memoir, *Unbridled*, Barbara McNally displays all these qualities and then some. Her adventuresome spirit, good humor, and fine writing make hers a journey you'll want to share.

—Judy Reeves, author of *A Writer's Book of Days*, www.judyreeveswriter.com

ADVANCE PRAISE FOR UNBRIDLED

Launching into new phases in her life, including the pain and discomfort as well as the freedom and joy of the venture, Barbara McNally communicates what many of us suspect—to be truly ourselves we might have to journey in directions we hadn't imagined. Gaining confidence, finding passion and a life's mission along with lessons from her ancestry, McNally is an example for those of us invested in making our lives meaningful. Moreover, she writes a great story. You'll feel with her every step of the way.

—Sheila Bender, author of A New Theology: Turning to
Poetry in a Time of Grief, www.writingitreal.com

What matters is not the destination, they tell us, but the journey. Whether the path we follow is a quest, a pilgrimage, or an exploration into memory, the ultimate journey can lead us into a deeper understanding of ourselves and our place in the world. Setting out on this odyssey requires courage, honesty, and a fair share of humility. In her memoir, Unbridled, Barbara McNally displays all these qualities and then some. Her adventuresome spirit, good humor, and fine writing make hers a journey you'll want to share.

—Judy Reeves, author of A Writer's Book of Days,
www.judyreeveswriter.com

Live.....

UNBRIDLED

Bob X McNally
June 18, 2013

UNBRIDLED

BARBARA McNALLY

BALBOA
PRESS
A DIVISION OF HAY HOUSE

Balboa Press books may be ordered through booksellers or by contacting:

Balboa Press
A Division of Hay House
1663 Liberty Drive
Bloomington, IN 47403
www.balboapress.com
1-(877) 407-4847

ISBN: 978-1-4525-6283-4 (sc)
ISBN: 978-1-4525-6282-7 (hc)

Library of Congress Control Number: 2012922160

Printed in the United States of America

Balboa Press rev. date: 02/27/2013

To my daughters.
May you be true to yourselves ... and dance!

Genuine inner freedom is the ultimate aim of life. It's the unspoken goal of every thought you have and every action you take.

—David Simon

CONTENTS

CONTENTS

AUTHOR'S NOTE

To round out my memories in writing this book, I relied on my personal journals and on conversations with those close to me. In all cases, my description of events represents my own perspective. Regarding my divorce, my attempt has been to present what I saw as irreconcilable differences without placing blame on either party. Twenty-three years of marriage changed me. Writing this book has allowed me to understand the impact and effects of those changes.

To preserve their anonymity, I have altered the names of many individuals who appear in this book.

ACKNOWLEDGMENTS

This book would not have been possible without the inspiration of Farrell Gallagher, who first prompted me to express myself on paper and supported me once I took that first bold step. I also am deeply indebted to fellow writers who helped shape my story by giving me honest feedback and constructive criticism. My heartfelt appreciation goes out to my editor, Jamie Winkelman, whose eagle eye and creative touch brought this manuscript to the next level with each revision (and there were many).

Thanks to Monkey C Media for the creative cover design and to J.T. MacMillan for the fabulous headshot.

My daughters deserve special recognition for their patience and understanding as I worked through this emotional project. More than once, they offered insight when my memory of events became selective. Finally, I'd like to thank my former husband for being a good provider, father, and teacher. Our marriage was a success. It just didn't last a lifetime.

Chapter 1

A LIAR AND A CHEATER

The tapered candles on the dining room table flickered in the evening's fading light. Surveying the table settings, I adjusted a fork and frowned when I noticed a smudge on one of the wine glasses. I plucked it up and polished it spotless with the flour-sack towel slung over my shoulder. With our older daughter, Molly, off at college and her sister, Kelly, overnighting at a friend's house to work on her eighth-grade history project, I was able to give my full attention to the dinner party my husband and I were hosting for some of his clients. Everything had to shine to perfection, including me.

One last sweep and I was finally satisfied with how it all looked. The florist had delivered fresh flowers, and several bottles of wine were chilling in the wine cooler. I'd prepared paella, my signature dish, which I'd learned to make during my college years when I'd volunteered at a physical therapy clinic in the Canary Islands.

I excelled at entertaining. Exalted in it. My mother had successfully taught Betty Crocker Barb how to set a stunning table, serve a delicious dinner, and pretend to be happy the entire time. According to my mother, life was all about appearances. She had married a politically conservative, Christian fundamentalist mining engineer. He was a steady provider and the antithesis of her wild and unpredictable parents. My mother once told me that he was as solid as the rocks he studied.

1

The rocks didn't interest her, but my father's rigidity did. In a way, I followed my mother's footsteps, carving out a stable life with someone as traditional as my father.

As the guests began to arrive at our Riverside, California, home, I set about making everyone comfortable, pouring champagne and passing canapés. Jay, "The Captain" as everyone called my husband, puffed out his chest like a rooster, planting kisses on the women's cheeks and glad-handing the men, slapping their backs in hearty camaraderie. Talk turned, as it always did, to how the goddamned liberals were ruining both our government and the moral fiber of our country. Eventually the conversation morphed into self-congratulatory boasts about financial deals and acquisitions. The women giggled and nodded at the pontificating males before starting up their own conversation about the latest shoe sale at Nordstrom. I watched the evening unfold, lost in my own thoughts. When did Jay and I become these people?

While the guests mingled in the living room, I took a moment in the kitchen to sip a glass of wine. I longed for the simplicity of the early eighties when Jay and I were first married. We had talked endlessly about our childhoods, our feelings, our dreams. We sprawled comfortably on the floor of our California condo, drinking cheap wine and spinning LPs on our new turntable. Over time, these conversations became ruminations on Italian leather sofas while we sipped collectible cabernets and listened to the latest musicians on our Bang & Olufsen stereo. To be fair, I enjoyed the art of living well, but as time went on, we began to place undue emphasis on the material details of our life together and not enough weight on the actual bond we shared—or didn't share.

I missed those days, but whenever I tried to resurrect our early talks and conversations about us, Jay snapped at me and made excuses about being under a lot of pressure at work. I probed for more information to understand what he was going through, but he refused to open up. I had a hard time with this. I needed to know him and believed he needed to know me. Otherwise, what was the point?

I had hoped we could renegotiate our floundering relationship and knock down the walls between us, but when that didn't work, I rebelled. The Irish fire in me burning, I snuck purchases and hid money, but retail therapy wasn't enough. I needed to feel wanted, desirable, necessary. I wanted to play an active role in our relationship, in my life. Earlier in our marriage, I had worked part-time as a physical therapist while Jay developed a home-building business. My income wasn't all that impressive, but working allowed me to maintain a sense of self. Once his company flourished, Jay preferred that I quit and stay at home with our daughters.

I didn't put up much of a fight. He led, and I followed.

Back then, I was afraid of confrontation. I also suffered from guilt. I thought that wanting more meant that I wasn't grateful for all Jay provided. The way I was raised, women should be taken care of without making demands of their own. Abiding by that idea made ours a parent-child relationship, not an adult marriage of equals.

The middle daughter of three, I was trim and athletic—and my father's overachieving tomboy. He coached my basketball and softball teams, and I glowed at his sideline encouragement. But after the balls were put away, he'd approach me with a laundry list of mistakes—the easy layup I'd missed, the botched catch. I was too slow. I was too fast. Nothing pleased him.

Eventually, I didn't need my father to torture me emotionally—I could do it myself. I could do it in my sleep. The criticism became a constant chant inside my head. I was never good enough in my own eyes, so how could I possibly be good enough for Jay? Still, every day I strove to make him happy, especially on Sundays.

Sunday meant golf and barbecue. And sex. It became mechanical, dutiful, and obligatory. I failed miserably when I tried to seduce Jay on a Tuesday or a Friday. Finally, desperately in fact, I tried to change things through reading.

"Listen to this, babe," I said one night, after he flicked off the bedroom television with his remote. I lay next to him, captivated by the *Kama Sutra*. "You won't believe how erotic these people were … thousands of years ago! Wanna try something different?"

He listened halfheartedly, then looked at me as if I had lost my mind. Barbie didn't experiment or exert her needs for pleasure; she did only what she was supposed to do to make her husband happy.

In the morning, searching for a way to reconnect, I attempted to persuade Jay to run away with me for a romantic weekend. I told him I'd bought tickets for a getaway to San Francisco.

"Well, let me call some of the guys. We'll make it a group vacation." He peered over the edge of his *Forbes* magazine, coffee in hand.

I smiled feebly and tried to get him to see my point. "Honey, I was thinking just the two of us," I said as I trailed my fingers up his arm. Jay jerked his hand back and flung the magazine down. He stormed over to the coffeemaker.

"Jesus Christ, not this again," he muttered, pouring himself a fresh cup.

"I thought it would be fun. A little one-on-one time."

"You're being selfish," he admonished, knowingly pushing my button. "Do you know how much work I have to do? I don't have time to go running off with you for two days."

My plan for a surprise getaway was a disaster. The tickets to San Francisco went unused.

Selfish was a code word. Eight years before, I'd stepped outside the confines of my marriage to find the attention and affection I needed. I had an affair, a textbook tryst complete with daylight dalliances in squalid motel rooms. Before our meetings, I felt drunk with desire—not only for my new lover, but also for whom I was when I was with him. But afterward, it was a different story. In the empty motel room, with the useless air conditioner cycling on and off again and the thick air smelling of mildew and sex, all the glamour and romance that had filled my heart deserted me. Feeling cheap and dirty, I tried to cleanse myself in the shower, but when I caught my reflection in the chipped mirror, an ugly witch glared back at me. A liar and a cheater. Ratty snarls knotted my hair, and makeup ran down my face. The tiny bar of soap crumbled in my hand as I tried to scrub away the scent of my lover and purge myself of my betrayal, vowing never to cheat again.

I swept my transgressions under the carpet and resumed the role of the dutiful wife, but I couldn't forgive myself. How could I forgive what I didn't understand—me? Confused and scared, I returned to where I knew it was safe, even if it was no longer fulfilling. Jay, meanwhile, knew I had been unfaithful, and although he acted like he had forgiven me, I knew he hadn't. I could tell by the way he tightened the matrimonial leash.

At the table, I fortified myself with more wine, as I served dinner and refreshed drinks. The conversation around the table droned on—business and politics. I knew better than to pipe in with my own opinion. Years earlier, I'd made the mistake of dropping a liberal viewpoint into one of these conservative-fests. Jay was irritated at me for being "disrespectful." His wife's political views should match his own, damn it, especially in front of clients. I didn't have the filters to express myself eloquently, so my opinions came off more bitchy than shrewd.

I let my focus drift out the picture window opposite our dining room. Tiny spotlights lit up the palm trees from below and cast a soft aura around the yard, transforming it into a world I yearned to explore. I missed the gratification of my career, helping others with the important tasks of day-to-day living. I craved discussions about philosophy, travel, and art. Anything but *this*.

I turned my eyes back to Jay, sitting at the other end of the table with his legs crossed in a casual but charismatic pose. He caught my gaze, then looked right through me, as if I were invisible. When everyone had finished eating, I stood and began to take away the dishes.

"Hey, Barb, let me help clear."

Sam stood at my elbow, a dinner plate in each hand. He was the only guest who'd come without a partner. His goatee matched his dirty-blond hair, and his white teeth were perfect, save for one on the bottom that jutted out a little.

"Oh, you don't have to do that," I said as I tried to add his plates to the ones I was already carrying. Sam sidestepped my attempt to take away his load and followed me into the kitchen.

"I'm sorry your girlfriend couldn't make it tonight," I said.

"Ex-girlfriend," he clarified, placing the dishes in the sink. Without looking up, he said, "You sure have been quiet tonight."

I stood there for a moment, poised to set out the meringues I'd prepared for dessert. I was shocked—and embarrassed—that someone had actually noticed me. Was my unhappiness that obvious?

I shrugged. "Oh, I've just been listening to what others say. You know how it is."

Sam chuckled. "Yeah. The conversation out there reminds me of dinner at my parents' house. I hate talking politics and finances."

I laughed in spite of myself. "You seemed like you were holding your own."

"Ah, well, you do what you have to when business is involved. Last year I took some time off and volunteered for Doctors Without Borders. They're always shorthanded when it comes to physicians. I heard that you and your daughter recently volunteered with Liga International."

"I knew we had something in common," I said, intrigued by the interests we shared.

Sam leaned toward me. I cocked my head as I caught a whiff of his cologne mixed subtly with the scents of the kitchen. Smitten, I fingered a tendril of hair that had escaped from my French twist.

"Would you be interested in coming along as a translator on our next medical mission to Mexico? You're fluent in Spanish, right? And you have a medical background," he said.

6

"My Spanish might be a little rusty. And I haven't worked as a physical therapist for years." I lowered my voice. "But I'd love to go on an adventure with you." I knew I wanted out of my situation, but I was surprised to hear myself sound so bold.

I laid my hand on his forearm. The bristles of his hair brushed against my fingertips, and I softly moved my fingers toward his bicep. He responded by touching the wrist of my other arm.

"Barb!" Jay boomed from the kitchen doorway. "The dessert?"

Sam cleared his throat and retreated to the dining room with a sheepish smile. I arranged little meringues on individual dessert plates, shame flooding my cheeks.

Sam and I avoided eye contact the rest of the night. After serving dessert, I poured coffee and Scotch, then busied myself with the evening's dishes. When I heard people begin to leave, I stepped out of the kitchen to say good-bye. Jay never spoke a word to me; he talked to the few stragglers until they, too, were ready to leave.

As soon as everyone was gone, I stole off to the bedroom, hoping to avoid the confrontation I knew was coming. I scrubbed my face clean of makeup and slipped into a nightgown before I crawled into bed and flipped on the television. I came across a program on the Dalai Lama—something Jay would never watch.

By the time he threw open the bedroom door, I was so engrossed in the show that I jumped when he came in. He wrenched the remote control out of my hand and, with a practiced flip, switched the channel to ESPN.

"Hey!" I said. "I was watching that."

Jay unbuttoned his Tommy Bahama shirt as if I hadn't even spoken. He shoved the remote in his pocket and strolled into our walk-in closet to hang up his shirt. I scrambled out of bed and ran after him, thrusting my hand in his pocket in search of the remote.

He brushed past me as he walked out of the closet. I followed him into the bathroom and held out my hand.

"I was watching something."

Jay splashed water against his face. "My TV."

"Can't I just watch a little goddamned TV? Didn't I just spend all day cleaning and cooking for your friends?"

"That's your job," he said as he dried his face. He walked to the bed.

"What? What's my job? To cater to you?" Barbie was out of her box and the anger was off and running.

"We've been through this before. I will not have a tramp for a wife."

"What am I supposed to do? Spend my life sitting around having boring conversations with your boring friends?"

"Sam's not so boring, is he?" Jay sniffed. His eyes tracked the sports feed along the bottom of the screen, but he had a different kind of score on his mind. "If I ever catch you doing anything like that again, I'll toss you out on your ass."

I drew up my shoulders and marched over to the front of the TV, blocking his view. He stared at me, his eyes ice.

"What the hell is wrong with you?" he asked, his voice monotone. "Did you have too much to drink?"

The truth was, I probably had. Or I hadn't had enough. Jay wasn't interested in my excuses. I shut down like a scolded child and didn't answer. There was no sense fighting back. Jay walked over to me. He placed his hands on my quivering shoulders and moved me a few inches to the right of the TV. Then he climbed into bed, turned off the lamp, and continued watching his game highlights while I stood there in the dark.

Hot tears of anger stung my eyes. I ran to the bathroom and slammed the door, where I collapsed against the sink and gripped the counter. I felt my world closing in.

———— ⚬⚬⚬ ————

As time went by, the frayed rope holding our marriage together continued to unravel. I distracted myself by raising my daughters and proudly watching them grow.

Kelly exhibited a passion for riding that equaled my own. We rode everyday and convinced Jay that a horse would be a good investment. He bought us a nine-year-old Arabian gelding named Money Talks. Then he washed his hands of all things horses.

Seeing Molly liberated by her first year at college, I was jealous. I wanted freedom, too. At the barn, the smell of rawhide, hay, sawdust, and sage brought back vivid memories of my childhood. As a young girl, I spent my allowance at the local stable. For me, jumping on a horse and going for a ride was the symbol of freedom from my authoritarian home life. It was the same as an adult. In the wide-open countryside, life was full of possibilities—and opportunities.

Carson, a hippie cowboy ten years my senior, was our trainer. He'd turned his back on teaching philosophy and given up the conventional life of an academic to train horses. His friends told me he was a Renaissance man gone horse whisperer. A talented competitor, he pushed the limits of reining events by riding his own course and by taking unbroken colts into the arena. Refusing to wear the conventional Wranglers and expensive Western shirts, he entered the show ring in no-name jeans and long-sleeved polos. He was a true original, not concerned with what others thought of him. The way he moved through his day intrigued me, and I felt comfortable dropping my pretenses around him.

Carson had worked with horses since childhood and never made much money at it, yet he seemed content with his life. He had a roof over his head and a few pennies in his pocket, and that was plenty. His indifference to the workaday world fascinated me. He moved at his own pace, as if he had only one gear. He didn't even wear a watch.

There was a peacefulness about him that attracted me. He could be in the moment without needing to perform, and I wanted to do the same. We shared an interest in Eastern religions, the teachings of the Dalai Lama, and the exploration of spirituality—all facets of my life in which Jay showed no interest. I read every book Carson suggested, soaking up the information.

"Try this one," he'd said, handing me *The Prophet*. I could imagine Jay scoffing at me as I turned its pages, which only made me more interested in the book. And in Carson.

Over the summer months of 2004, Carson and I galloped through the orange groves, resting under fragrant trees. We munched on peanut butter–and–jelly sandwiches made with squishy white bread and talked about horses, philosophy, and life. One day, while Kelly was at school, I shared the troubles I was having in my marriage, how I struggled over whether I should stay.

Carson leaned back against a tree, peeling an orange while he spoke. "You see that cocoon hanging right there?" he asked, pointing with a dripping wedge of orange. "The caterpillar that used to live there has outgrown the cocoon that was once its home. It left the safety of that place to become a butterfly. It wasn't an easy thing to do, but if the caterpillar had stayed, it would have died. Right now, you are like that caterpillar."

He was right.

Nearly a year after Kelly and I started riding with him, Carson invited our family to Paso Robles during Kelly's spring break to watch him show Money Talks at the annual reining competition. Since he was an accomplished rider, he stood a good chance of winning. Molly was in Mexico for her first college getaway, so Kelly invited her friend Suzanne. Jay, of course, declined to go. I suspect the only reason he allowed me to attend was so that I could chaperone Kelly and Suzanne on an out-of-town overnight.

I had never vacationed on California's Central Coast and was eager to get out of Riverside. I packed up the girls in the SUV and drove north. At the competition, the warm days passed with a full schedule of events: rollbacks, sliding stops, and spins. When Saturday evening came, high-intensity lamps bathed the arena in light. Kelly, Suzanne, and I sat in the bleachers and cheered with each progressive round that Carson won astride Money Talks. When he accepted the championship buckle, I raced down the metal bleachers, my boots landing loudly with each step. I threw my arms around a sweaty Carson, and we embraced in a congratulatory hug that lasted a little longer than it should have.

Carson gave me the number of his room in the motel across the street from mine and invited me to celebrate with a nightcap. As soon as the girls were safely tucked away in their own room, I snuck out. I knew I was playing with fire, but I was hundreds of miles from home. I couldn't possibly get caught.

That night, Carson and I crossed the line between trainer and trainee. We were both teachers, and we were both students.

I woke to find the sky tinged with shades of dawn. I glanced around for a clock, and finding none, reluctantly kicked away the sheets and walked over to the dresser. I reached into my purse to check the time on my phone.

"Shit." Stupid me. I had left my cell phone in my motel room. I could picture it sitting on the nightstand. "I gotta go," I said, yanking on my jeans and boots, memories from my previous infidelity flooding back.

When I slipped into my room, I heard my phone chirping. Eight missed calls and three new messages. In the first, Jay unleashed a barrage of insults at me about what a slut I was. The second voicemail described my deplorable qualities as an unfit mother. In the third, he informed me he'd be making the five-hour drive to pick up the girls as soon as he hung up. I checked the time stamp of the last message. Over an hour had passed. I took a deep breath and dialed.

"I'll meet you at home," I said in a rush. "I'm on my way now, and I'll explain when I get there."

I clicked off my phone and jumped at the knock on my hotel room door. When I opened it, Kelly stood there in tears, her face red and puffy. Suzanne stood next to her with an uncertain look on her face. She was crying, too.

"I didn't know what to do, Mom. I saw you leave, and you didn't come back. And then you didn't answer when I tried to call. I thought something happened."

Something did happen.

I fucked up.

Again.

———※———

When I pulled into the driveway, Jay was pacing in the front yard. The girls quickly got out of the car and went inside. I stalled, then slowly opened the driver's door.

"I'm done," he said, his face hard with humiliation and hostility. We stood there, frozen in an awkward silence that seemed impossible between two once happily married people. Jay never took his eyes off me.

"I'm sorry," I said, my voice faltering. He knew I'd been unfaithful again, and I didn't make any attempt to deny it. I wanted him to know me, accept me, love me, but I had really screwed things up.

"Our marriage is over," he said, his tone matter-of-fact. The rage that had sizzled through the phone lines a few hours before had burned itself out. "We still have half our lives ahead of us. We should give ourselves a chance to find someone more compatible to share what's left."

He bent down and took my head in his huge hands, gripping my skull with his fingertips. Our faces were inches apart, and he locked his eyes with mine like a father looking at his daughter, sad and wistful in the moment when he realizes that she has made a mistake.

His kindness surprised me, but I knew. It was over.

"I've always taken care of you," he said. "It's hard for me to believe that you're going to be on your own. How will you ever make it? You're still a child."

When he released me, I dropped my gaze and shrugged in defeat and fear. I'd gone from my father's house to Jay's and never been alone.

"So I guess this is it then," I said. I wiped away tears with the sleeve of my shirt and swallowed hard. "I'll start looking for a place this weekend."

More out of habit than anything, I suppose, we slept in the same bed that night. Sometime during the middle of the night, he mounted me, as if to claim his property. Part of me wanted to be reclaimed, but I pretended to resist his aggressiveness, yelping as he grabbed at me and pinned one of my wrists to the bed. I tried to hit him with my free arm, but he jerked away. For the first time in a long time, we had hot, passionate sex.

He loved me, he hated me. He loved me, he hated me. Barbie had torched the dream house, and Ken was on the rampage. I was *his*, damn it. He hated me for changing that. I hated myself for hurting the man I once loved.

When he rolled off me, I felt more than his weight lift from my body. He fell into a deep sleep a few minutes later, and heaving snores escaped from his mouth.

I got up and locked myself in the bathroom. I cried over what had just happened and for what could have been. Then I cried for forgiveness. Cried for the death of our marriage. Cried for Molly and for Kelly. And finally, I cried out of fear of being alone.

I huddled in a tiled corner, curled in the fetal position until I finally fell into a fitful sleep. I woke in the middle of the night when I heard Jay rattling the doorknob, demanding to come in so he could use the toilet. After a few unanswered twists, I heard him shuffle down the hall to the guest bathroom. Holding the edge of the counter, I brought myself to my feet and flipped on the light. My face was swollen and wrinkled from where it had been pressed up against the edge of the tub. Whether it was a cheap motel room or million-dollar home, the guilt and shame were exactly the same.

I was trapped in a cage of my own making. It was up to me to find my way out of the mess. The door had slammed shut on the life I'd once known, and I had no idea what it was going to look like on the other side.

Chapter 2

DEPARTURES

I packed a small bag and set it by the front door. Spring break was over, and Molly would be going back to school soon. Jay and I probably should have sat down together with our teenage girls and explained to them that we just couldn't be married anymore. That it was about us, not them, that even though their father and mother would be apart, we would both continue to be there for them.

But Jay had already left for work, and the girls and I were sitting around the kitchen table eating cold cereal. Should I wait until dinner to break the news? After dinner? Before they went to bed? The occasional clank of a spoon interrupted the monotonous hum of the refrigerator, but other than that, it was uncomfortably quiet. I cleared my throat.

"I'm staying at Jean's tonight. After that, I'll probably pack up the rest of my things and move out. Please believe me when I tell you it has nothing to do with you girls."

They both stopped eating and looked at me as if I had told them that I only had a short time to live. The guilt and remorse I felt for breaking up our family caused me more anguish than I could articulate. The way I was raised, you just didn't "do" divorce. You hung on to the cliff until your hands were bloody and raw; you suffered in silence. But by living the lie of a happily married wife, I had sold my soul.

I convinced myself that Carson was more than just my lover—he was my soul mate. It was easier for me to justify my sins when I thought we would ride off together into the sunset.

Soon after I moved out, I sought an attorney's professional counsel and filed for divorce. The attorney served Jay with the divorce papers at his workplace, and Jay didn't waste any time. When I retuned home for my things I found all the family pictures that had hung on our walls piled up on the front steps. What had I done? How could I hurt the man I once loved? What were the ramifications going to be?

The following week, the locks were changed. Scared and alone, I sat outside the front door crying. I don't know how long I stayed there. Eventually, I pulled myself together and began to assess my future.

It turned out that dissolving our marriage was easier than holding it together. To make things simpler for the girls, Jay and I both wanted to get things over with quickly. I surrendered without a fight to gain my freedom instead of battling in court with an emotional, drawn-out proceeding. I moved out of "his" house and didn't go after "his" business. We split our personal assets and shared equal custody of the girls.

Over the next few months, I enjoyed being able to spend more time with Carson, freely and openly. I felt less guilt, but I still felt it. Even so, I was beginning to collect memories not regrets. We shared conversations and experiences that I wanted to hold on to.

Falling in love was intoxicating. When I sobered up, however, I realized that, while Carson and I had come into our relationship for a reason, our season had passed. I wanted to be free. He had opened the gate, and my spirited horse wanted to explore many trails, not be corralled back into another stable.

But still feeling guilty about breaking up my family, I had no idea what to do with my freedom. That's when my friend Jean stepped in. She put it to me plain and simple.

"You need someone to help you sort through all this emotional wreckage. No offense, Barb, but I don't think your family qualifies. You need to find a professional who can help you. It's amazing how we think nothing of seeking out attorneys and financial planners to help us deal with the practical aspects of divorce and never get help with the emotional ones."

I wasn't convinced. Therapy was for crazy people, and I was wary about carving yet another brand into my flesh. The scarlet letter and the big *D* seemed quite enough for one year. My load was already heavy. I didn't need to add the social stigma of therapy.

"Relax, Barb. He's easy to talk to. He's not going to tell you what to do or give you all the answers. He'll help you find your own answers."

I finally agreed to give it a try. When I mentioned to my mother that I planned to go into therapy, she gave me a puzzled look. "Why dear? Are you sick?"

The day of my first appointment, I arrived twenty minutes early and sat in my car, staring at the old house that had been converted into an office. Was I strong enough to bare my soul in front of a complete stranger? Maybe I didn't need a therapist after all. I sat a few minutes longer, fidgeting with my keys, rearranging my glove box, before I got out and walked through the white door into the office. If it didn't work out, I didn't have to come back, but I was willing to give it a shot.

I was the only person in the waiting room, which was originally the living room. I filled out all the necessary forms the receptionist handed me, grateful for the distraction. After what seemed like an eternity, she ushered me in to see the therapist. I stopped when I saw him. He was just a regular guy, dressed in tan corduroy pants and a blue polo shirt, not a disheveled clinician wearing a wrinkled white coat and waving a ticking pendulum. His watery blue eyes and the touch of gray at his temples put me at ease.

He stood up from his tattered wing-backed chair and held out his hand. "Hello," he said. "I'm Dr. Gallagher. You can call me Farrell. Please have a seat."

I sat uncomfortably on the edge of the chair that matched the one he had been sitting in. I was afraid that if I sat any farther back in the dished-out cushion, I might never get up. I looked around self-consciously at the walls. A small painting portrayed a peaceful lake with wildflowers in the foreground and jagged mountains behind. Above the door, thick drops of hardened paint spilled between the grates of the heater vent. Farrell returned to his seat and crossed one leg over the other, adjusting his pant leg to cover his sock.

"How are you?" he asked.

"I don't know why I'm here," I said, waiting for a response. Farrell just listened. "I mean I know why I'm here, but I don't know what I'm supposed to say." I looked around at the shelves of books and the stacks of journals lying on his desk.

"Say whatever you feel."

I didn't say anything. Couldn't. Until the silence became too much.

"I just got a divorce."

"Would you like to talk about that?"

It was as if he'd tugged on an errant strand of yarn from my sweater. I fell apart, loose and unraveled. Tears streaked my face, and the layers of masks peeled away. Farrell pushed a box of tissues toward me.

"I feel like I just jumped out of a burning building and I'm free-falling. I couldn't be myself in my marriage, and now I'm scared of being alone."

I told Farrell everything, from how Jay and I met, to the affairs, to the inevitable and bitter end. I watched his face for judgment, but none came. That comforted and encouraged me even more. When I had unloaded my story, I sat back and waited for him to speak.

"You got caught with two affairs. It would seem to me that you wanted out of the marriage. You made it hard to get back in." His voice was soothing and compassionate. He twirled his pen.

"If I hadn't, the leash would have been so tight, it would have choked me. I'd be more of a prisoner than a partner."

"It's cruel to stay with someone you don't love," Farrell said. "To stay would have been selfish. He doesn't want you back. In the end, you made sure of that. Let him be free to find someone more compatible with who he is and what he needs."

For a moment, I felt like Farrell was siding with Jay. It didn't seem fair since I was the one seeking help. I tried to formulate my thoughts into words that would justify my actions.

"It's ironic. I was raised to be kind, but lately I feel like no matter what I do, I'm selfish and I hate that." I leaned back into my chair, sinking deeply into the seat. "I wanted him to be different. I wanted him to change." Outside the window, a sudden breeze dislodged the purple petals of a jacaranda tree, and I watched them float to the ground. A fly buzzed against the window, trying to escape.

"Yes, but the problem is you can't change him. The only person you can change is yourself."

"But I wasn't valued for who I was—I was valued for the roles I played. The man I was married to for twenty-three years never really knew me." I laid my cheek in an open palm and stared at the carpet. "I feel like I have a split personality, like I have all these different dimensions to myself even though I wasn't able to live out these roles in my marriage."

Farrell set down his pen and drew his fingers into a steeple under his chin, waiting for me to continue. I settled into the chair, increasingly comfortable with the mild-mannered man. I rambled in a stream of consciousness, with no connective tissue binding my words.

"I just can't stop feeling guilty. I decimated my marriage, destroyed my family. I don't know what I'm going to do about my daughters. They may never forgive me for ruining their lives and breaking apart the only home they've ever known." I recognized that Jay and I were both responsible for the failure of our marriage, but talking so openly about my guilt made me seem more at fault. And it made me wonder if I had done the right thing by leaving.

"Were you an equal partner in your marriage? Did you feel loved? And most of all, did you feel respected?" Farrell asked.

"No, no, and no."

"The strength of a relationship is based on the degree of shared reality, rather than the position of wife, mother, sister, or daughter. You have to ask yourself, 'What do I love? What excites me? Inspires me? Who do I idolize?'"

Farrell gave voice to the questions I had thought I had no right to even ask, let alone answer. Sitting there, I realized that answering those questions was an important step toward discovering who I really was. But I didn't have the answers. Not yet, anyway.

"Don't let other people do your thinking for you," he continued. "You're not born empty-headed. There is a soul within you. It's up to you to bring that soul to life, express who you are."

I took a deep breath and tried to digest everything he had said. We'd covered a lot of ground since I walked through his door. I'd bared my soul, and he had started to show me how to view it.

He glanced at the clock above my head. "Time's up, but we can pick up where we left off next week, if you'd like."

We did. And we picked up again the next week. And the next. I went into therapy with the notion that the therapist would fix me. Instead, he gave me permission to explore and accept who I was—my complexities and even my contradictions. He helped me go inside myself to excavate my own answers from beneath the rubble of my life. I was free to make my own choices and to take responsibility for my own life. I was learning that relationships come and go—and when that happens, one person generally leaves before the other person is ready. Over time, I saw that I was the captain of my own ship. But when I sailed in unchartered waters, I recognized the value of good navigators.

I was driving home from Kelly's high school soccer game when my cell phone rang. I glanced at the caller ID. It was my mother. My heart rate spiked. She never called me on my cell.

"Hi, Mom. What's up?"

"Honey, your grandma just died."

She didn't preface her announcement by saying she had something to tell me. She didn't ask if I was sitting down. She just said it, and I nearly crashed.

Swerving for the nearest stopping point, I pulled into a vacant parking lot. The oppressive heat of the Riverside smog made my head spin. Nearby warehouses and strip centers were blanketed in a filmy haze that masked the mountains in the distance. I drew in a deep breath and exhaled.

"So, are you okay?" I asked, once I found my voice. Even though my mother had never been close to Grandma Pat, she was still her daughter.

"Yes," she replied. I could hear the strain in her response. "She died peacefully, and she lived a full life."

That was an understatement.

Two weeks later, I sprawled on Mom's floor with photos of Grandma Pat strewn around me in a ragged semicircle. An entire life scattered in little piles. I picked up a curled black-and-white print, holding it by the scalloped edges. The back was annotated in neat handwriting with her given name. Pauline, age 10. She was kneeling demurely in a long, white Communion dress, her dark hair pulled back to reveal an alabaster face with a mischievous expression that said, "I may look like an angel now, but watch out world, here I come!"

I reached for another photo, a larger one of Grandma and Grandpa from their elopement. The dark border made it look as if it had once been framed. Grandma Pat, nicknamed "Cat Eyes" by my grandfather, sported a fringed flapper dress and a sexy feathered hat. She may have looked the part of a young bride, posing in front of the shiny Model T Ford and holding her wedding bouquet, but there was nothing demure about those huge green eyes. They sparkled with a look that was feisty and utterly unafraid.

My mother's relationship with her wild and unpredictable mother had always been tense. They were both pretty, but—unlike Grandma Pat—Mom lived to please others, conforming at all costs. Since appearances were important to her, she always had a smile on her face, even if she was crying on the inside. Her conservative outfits matched her personality, as did her home with its country French décor. Prim, proper, and always impeccable. My mother took after Grandma Pat's five sisters—the ones who lived as modest, subservient wives in conventional marriages.

Grandma Pat was the first woman in her family to go to college. She earned tuition money by working in a candy shop, where she met Harold Robinson, a suave cigarette salesman and polished bootlegger who had his eye on a different kind of sweet. They eloped a month after they met. The eighteen-year-old bride clipped her long black hair into a trendy bob and shortened her name to Pat. She shed everything that might drag her back to the farm where she grew up.

Looking at the photos stirred up my memories of Grandma Pat drinking tea (sometimes with a shot of Irish whiskey) and telling stories about my Celtic Irish heritage. In Gaelic, whiskey means "water of life," so it seemed appropriate that Grandma Pat spiked her tea with the amber spirits. Her stories left me yearning for a lifestyle like hers, a sense of adventure. Even though I was raised during the women's lib movement of the sixties and seventies, the only movers and shakers I heard about at home were Billy Graham and Anita Bryant. The fundamental Baptist lifestyle adopted by my parents stifled liberal views such as racial tolerance, premarital sex, and—God forbid—gay rights.

It seemed as if the dynamic era of the twenties had been tailor-made for Grandma Pat. She danced with the fun-loving flapper girls on Friday nights and marched with the serious-minded suffragettes on Saturday mornings. While the suffragettes viewed the flappers as frivolous—dancing instead of marching—Grandma Pat boasted that she balanced both worlds with ease. Staring at her pictures, I felt the power of being a woman and wondered why I had failed to live an equally honest and liberated life.

Among Grandma Pat's effects were pictures of the vaudeville theater she and Grandpa Harold ran in Carlyle, Illinois. I remembered the glittery childhood fantasies I'd had about live music, slapstick comedy, and burlesque. Sitting on the floor, I imagined a young Grandma Pat dancing like Gypsy Rose Lee or Sally Rand, doing the comedic and artful tease that these women were so famous for. I lifted a photo of my smiling grandparents square dancing and wondered how I had lost the playfulness in my marriage. Where had it gone? Or had it ever really been there?

After years of the vaudeville life, my grandparents had shifted gears and moved to Arizona to start a family. Grandpa Harold and Grandma Pat sold real estate and raised my mother—their only child—but they never lost their zest for life.

My grandparents visited often when I was growing up. They interrupted my parents' regimented lifestyle with an energetic and rambunctious flair. One time when they were in town, my mom attempted to save Grandma Pat's soul. Three generations of females were sitting around the kitchen table after dinner.

"Which church are you attending these days?" my mother asked Grandma Pat.

"I'm not," she said, sipping her whiskey-fortified tea. "Church is for hypocritical conformists."

"Jesus loves you no matter who you are or what you have done," Mom said, seemingly unfazed by the accusation. "Believe in him, accept him into your heart, and you will have eternal life in heaven."

"Go to hell."

I sat in the chair next to Grandma Pat and stared at the teapot in the middle of the table, desperately trying not to laugh. My sisters looked at each other uncomfortably, wide-eyed in shock at Grandma Pat's audacity.

More than once, I wondered if my mother was adopted. It didn't seem possible that feisty, vivacious Grandma Pat could have had such a God-fearing June Cleaver for a daughter. But to my mother's credit, she never tried to shield me from my grandmother or contradict the things Grandma Pat told me about life.

When Grandpa Harold died in his seventies, his death didn't slow down Grandma Pat, who was nine years younger. I met the boyfriends she traveled with after my grandfather's death. There were plenty of them, most much younger than she was. Bold, passionate, and sensual, she embodied a lifestyle quite contrary to the environment in which I grew up. I wasn't even allowed to watch films like *Love Story*, but— much to my parents' dismay—being around my grandmother made me curious about my own sexuality.

It broke my heart when an aging Grandma Pat phoned to say that she was moving into a new "home." I could hear the pain and humiliation in her voice when she told me that she needed help, that she couldn't make it on her own anymore. Admitting this was probably the hardest thing she ever did. It was a sad conversation that I remembered well, one I hoped never to have with my own children.

Reluctantly, Grandma Pat moved into an assisted-living facility near my parents in Carlsbad. Whenever my mother and I went to visit her, Mom would briefly say hello and then adjourn to the visitors' lounge. Dealing with the thought of death was just too painful for her. In contrast, I took the creep of death as my impetus to learn all I could from Grandma Pat.

While I'd brush her long hair, which was always dyed jet-black, I listened to her stories of our ancestors in Ireland, wondering if my two sisters related to Grandma Pat the way I did. Brea and Mary were carbon copies of my mother—at the opposite end of the spectrum from my grandmother, who didn't judge and seemed to see the good in everyone, no matter how different they were or where they stood in life. I believed my grandmother and I shared a certain spark and energy, that we were kindred spirits. I never thought she'd be gone, despite the frailty of her old age. But she was. Dead at ninety-two, beautiful until her last day.

Grandma Pat had always encouraged me to create the life I wanted and not worry about what people might say: "Ten percent will applaud you, ten percent will condemn you, and the rest won't give a damn because they're living their own lives." She was so independent, it didn't seem like she ever needed anything from anyone. I guess my mother got the same impression, because she went through Grandma Pat's death arrangements as if she were marking off a grocery list. She didn't have a funeral service to honor her mother. She was sure Grandma Pat was burning in hell.

As I sat on my mother's living room floor and sifted through the pile of photographs, I noticed a plain manila envelope without any markings. When I opened it, out tumbled photographs I'd never seen before. All of Grandma Pat—and she wasn't wearing any clothes.

"Mom!" I shouted.

"What is it?" she asked, returning from the kitchen with two cups of tea.

"Look!"

In hindsight, I should have prepared her for what she was about to see. My mother was a woman who kept her house as sterile as a hospital because she worried what the neighbors might think. I knew she wouldn't like what I'd found. After all, it's not every day someone sticks a photo of your naked mother in your face. Besides, they weren't old black-and-white flapper photos from the Roaring Twenties; they were color-saturated foreplay pictures from the Swinging Seventies.

"Oh my heavens!"

My mother's hands trembled as she set down the teacups and seized the photo. Grandma Pat lay sprawled across a bed with a strategically placed white feather boa. She had struck a pose she'd probably assumed a thousand times in her dancing days. But it was too much for my mother.

"What was she thinking? This is just ..."

"Amazing?" I suggested.

"Awful!"

There were at least a dozen more of these photographs. Grandpa had died when I was still in high school, so one of Grandma Pat's boyfriends must have taken the pictures. Although she was probably in her sixties, she still looked beautiful. She had robust breasts, an athletic body, and hair that fell to her waist. Her big green eyes told the story. She had the look of a woman who was proud of who she was. But where I saw a woman who was confident in herself and comfortable with her body, my mother saw something completely different. She blushed at the brazen way Grandma Pat had bared her breasts for the camera and the seductive manner in which the feather boa snaked between her legs.

"Oh, Mom, lighten up," I said. "She looks great. And kudos to her for having the courage to express herself."

"Well, I'm not keeping them," she said as she gathered the racy photos into a pile and grabbed a nearby wastebasket.

"You can't throw these away. You act like there's something wrong with a woman embracing her sexuality!" My mother looked at me as if I had taken leave of my senses. She shook her head, tightening her thin Irish lips and glaring at me.

"Fine," she snapped. "Just get them out of here where I can't see them."

She thrust the pictures at me, as though she might catch a communicable disease by touching them. Grandma Pat had lived almost a century, yet even in death, she never gained the approval of her own daughter.

My mother retired to her bedroom, and I kept sorting through the photographs, arranging them into piles—for my mother, my two sisters, and me. In the last envelope, I found an embossed napkin, a few faded postcards of Ireland, rosary beads, and a small journal. Artifacts from Grandma Pat's travels. I fingered the rosary beads and wondered why she had kept them all those years even though she'd left the Catholic Church in her youth. Flipping through the pages of the journal, I read Grandma Pat's hand-scrawled notes about Eastern religions and quotes from ancient philosophers, things I had no idea she was interested in—a testament to her open-mindedness. The words "I'm a Mother, Lover, Fighter, and Saint" jumped off the page.

But as exciting as those finds were, I kept returning to the photographs of Grandma Pat in the buff. I was struck by her boldness, how happy she looked. She was not a woman encumbered with worries about what others might think, nor waiting for someone to give her a blessing. I thought of all the things she would have missed out on if she had cared what others thought—and all the opportunities I'd let slip through my fingers because I cared too much. I felt a curious twinge of shame for allowing myself to become a timid, fearful person who lived in the shadow of others.

Grandma Pat was an open book. She lived life on her own terms and apologized to no one. Even so, she was kind and thoughtful. The racy photographs I found weren't evidence of a secret life. Grandma Pat had kept them hidden in consideration of my mother's feelings; she wouldn't embarrass her daughter. I wondered if she knew that one day those same photos would inspire me. There was no doubt that Grandma Pat was special, but I was determined to not let the qualities I admired so much die with her.

—※—

If it hadn't been for those bold photographs of Grandma Pat, I don't think I would have struck out alone toward the shores of a faraway country.

During the twenty-three years of my marriage, I'd been content to

27

let my husband plan all of our family vacations. And plan he did—down to the very last detail. This time, Jay would not be sitting beside me, hogging the armrest and putting his stuff on my tray table. I'd booked my flight at the last minute. I was going to see Ireland, the land of my ancestors—hardworking farmers who tilled the soil, pirate queens who plundered the coastline, and emigrants to America who performed as entertainers, including Grandma Pat, the inspiration for my journey.

I would be flying solo, spontaneously embarking on something new. I didn't know what to call what I was doing. I wasn't even sure it had a name. A vacation? A voyage?

It couldn't be the former as I didn't have any fun activities planned, and the latter sounded too serious, too nineteenth century. A voyage was what my ancestors undertook to leave Ireland to make a new life in America—sailing in coffin ships full of their starving countrymen, fighting off hunger, scurvy, and yellow fever. I was on a trip to rediscover myself by going back to my roots. It was a re-creation of the person I longed to become, a rebirth.

My daughters would say I was freaking out, and they'd be right. I hadn't booked a hotel room or reserved a rental car. I didn't even know how long I'd be gone. They pestered me for information about where I was staying and with whom. I reassured them I was traveling alone, which didn't reassure them in the least. I had to explain that I wasn't running off to Ireland forever, just for a few weeks while they were on vacation with their father. Beyond that, I didn't really know. I was touched by their concern, but it felt like a role reversal. I realized that their anxiety went deeper than wondering if I'd be okay or when I'd be returning home. They didn't know what to expect from me anymore. And, in all honesty, neither did I.

I wanted to show my true self to my daughters, but like a gay person coming out of the closet, I wasn't sure they would accept me for who I was. My girls were growing up, becoming young women, and—at the risk of losing their love—I was afraid to be frank with them. For too many years, fear of rejection had kept me in hiding. I wanted to strip away the deceit and get rid of all my lies, but what if they didn't understand?

Whatever magic had created that energetic unit we once called "family" had abandoned us. Shortly after my divorce, I rented a small house near where Kelly would start high school. The girls were still angry with me for leaving Jay. They saw firsthand the pain it caused him and couldn't believe anyone—let alone their own mother—would do this to their father. Since I was the one in motion, and Jay was the one standing still, they figured I had ruined everything. After all, their father hadn't gone anywhere. It had to be me who was the problem.

—⁂—

I dodged other passengers at Los Angeles International Airport, muttering about their snail-like pace, and reached the gate out of breath. For the third time in as many minutes, I checked my watch. When I glanced at the departure board, I sighed in relief and frustration. I wasn't late after all. I was an hour early. I hadn't even known what time my flight was supposed to leave.

Aside from a vague notion of going to Westport, the small coastal town in County Mayo where my great-great-grandmother Bridget O'Dwyer was born, I didn't have a plan. No timetables or itineraries, no maps or travel guides to follow. I'd figure it out when I got there. I had always cared too much about what others thought, seeking approval from my father and my husband—even (some would say, especially) when it was unrealistic to expect it. At last, I was free to do as I pleased.

Agitated by my pretravel jitters, I silently wished for insight and inspiration from Grandma Pat, who always seemed confident about what she wanted and went after it without looking back. Her guidance came to me in a fond memory of her sage advice: "Barbara, I don't know the meaning of life, but it's not a popularity contest. Make decisions based on what is right for you, not somebody else." I hadn't taken this to heart when I first heard it. But waiting for my flight to Ireland, it made perfect sense. Wasn't that why I was going?

I found a place to sit among my fellow travelers and went down my mental checklist: boarding pass, passport, wallet, handbag, magazines. Everything I needed for a flight across the Atlantic. I was ready to begin my journey into the unknown.

"Headed to Ireland are you?"

I was so deep in my thoughts, I barely heard the question. The handsome, dark-haired man across from me had blue eyes, a lanky frame, and spoke with a lilt that betrayed he was from the Emerald Isle. I smiled and nodded. He got up, stuck out his hand, and introduced himself as Casey. Soon he was chatting away about how much he was looking forward to going back to the Irish countryside and seeing his family again. Then he started peppering me with questions.

"What part of the country will you be visiting? Do you have family there? Are you traveling alone? Why Ireland?"

Casey was so frank and open (my mother would have said forward) that I wanted to answer his questions, but I didn't quite know how. I didn't know where I was going, and my knowledge of my family's roots was scattershot at best. I didn't want Casey to think I was some clueless American tourist who was going to ride around on a stuffy tour bus and snap photographs of the countryside through half-opened windows. I wanted him to understand why visiting his country meant so much to me, but I didn't have the words. It didn't escape me that I was still struggling to meet the expectations of others, even those I didn't know. I was trapped beneath a mask that always made me look good.

As the gate attendant made the first boarding call for Flight 1959, connecting to Shannon, I dug into my purse for the photo of Grandma Pat and handed it to Casey.

"This is why I'm going."

Casey accepted the photo with a guarded smile. He probably

thought he was getting a funeral card or some dingy portrait of a distant ancestor. But one look at my naked Grandma Pat and Casey's eyes lit up.

"And who's this?"

"My grandmother."

"Well now," he said, handing the photo back to me. His face turned blotchy with a heated flush of what I guessed was part arousal and part embarrassment. "If you're anything like your grandmother, you won't have any trouble making friends."

Chapter 3

ARRIVALS

I n the early 2000s, the Celtic Tiger began to roar for the first time
since the Potato Famine. Irish men and women no longer left Ireland
to find work; instead, they stayed home in record numbers. More people
were coming to visit Ireland than were leaving it, and I was part of that
diaspora in reverse. Shaking off the shackles of my marriage and the
ultraconservative life it had entailed, I looked to Ireland as a salve for
my wounded spirit. Visiting the land of my ancestors seemed like the
perfect tool for me to figure out who I was and, more importantly, who
I wanted to become.

I was embarking on a journey of redemption. I had a feeling that
if I traveled back through the archways of history, I might find in my
Irish ancestors some reflection of my lost self, some thread that I could
carry into the future. Ireland was the best of both worlds—completely
foreign and new to me, but also deeply embedded in my DNA. I
believed that, on the Emerald Isle, I could tap into something primal,
mysterious, and true.

"In preparation for landing, please ensure that your seat belts are
securely fastened and that your seat backs and tray tables are in their
upright and locked positions."

I woke with a start, my fingers clutching at my seat belt. I was
obediently buckled in. I'd drifted off to sleep and dreamed I was on

a journey, traveling not on an airplane but aboard a creaking ship, crashing through the waves and across the sea. As we approached the harbor, a wall of fog rose up and prevented us from pulling into port. The captain turned the ship this way and that, but it was no use. The harder he tried to penetrate the fog, the farther away we drifted. I clutched the rails, expecting to crash into a jetty or another vessel, listening for the sound of rocks ripping open the hull. So as the wheels of the airplane touched down and skipped along the asphalt, my heart skipped right along with them.

I looked out the window. The countryside was socked in with low clouds. I felt queasy with anticipation and, truth be told, more than a touch of fear. Generations before me, my great-great-grandmother had left Ireland with a profound hunger in her belly. Now, I had come to my homeland with a different kind of hunger. But unlike my ancestors, I had a return ticket in my handbag. If I ran into trouble or had a change of heart, I could jump on a plane that would speed me back home any time I wanted. It made me appreciate both the sacrifices the women in my family had made and the opportunity I had before me.

I moved through the throngs of people at Shannon Airport to the baggage claim carousel, smiling at reassembled families and reunited lovers. As I waited for my bags, my ears rang with the sound of the native tongue. I tried to eavesdrop on the conversations around me, but I wasn't accustomed to the musical lilt of their voices and the speed with which they spoke. It wasn't until the crowds thinned out and the bags were all gone that I realized my luggage wasn't on the carousel.

At the baggage-claim office, I got my first real dose of a County Clare brogue. The gentleman talked a mile a minute—make that a *kilometer* a minute. It didn't matter, because I couldn't understand half the things he said. I showed him my baggage-claim ticket and squinted at him in hopes of better understanding the words pouring out of his mouth. Finally, he grasped that I couldn't understand him. He shook his head from side to side. That I understood: My bags were missing. Apparently, I'd made the trip without them.

"They're gone?" I took another look at my claim check, as if that might make my luggage magically appear.

"Aye, we'll call ya."

"Call me where?"

"Where are ya staying, luv?" he asked.

"I don't know."

It was his turn to look at me quizzically.

"I haven't settled on a place yet."

"Where would ya be headed now?"

"I don't know that either."

He raised his eyebrows then pointed to a laminated map, colorfully embellished with icons identifying Irish landmarks. "This may help ya some," he said. "Give us a call when ya find a place to stay, and we'll ring ya when the bags are found."

Judging from his expression, he thought I was as lost as my luggage. Maybe I was.

I nodded and looked down at the handbag—my only bag—that contained my passport, wallet, and travel toothbrush. I began to curse my impulsivity, my lack of foresight, my capriciousness. I should have planned ahead. But then I thought of my great-great-grandmother, Bridget, and how little she must have had when she left for America. Like most emigrants, she was poor—desperately so. I wasn't going to let a minor inconvenience like lost luggage slow me down. Surely I could pick up some knock-around clothes to hold me over until my bags turned up. I took down the phone number for the baggage-claim office and proceeded to the rental car counter.

Just as I hadn't made any hotel reservations, I had neglected to hire a car. No, "neglected" suggests that I forgot or failed to reserve a vehicle. Nothing of the sort. Not reserving a car was part of my plan to not have a plan. Remembering the look the man at the baggage-claim office had given me, I started to have second thoughts.

One after another, the representatives from the rental car agencies told me how sorry they were that they couldn't help me. Of course there weren't any cars—it was peak tourist season. Besides being the perfect time to visit Ireland, they explained, August was the month when most Europeans went on holiday. My cheeks burned with embarrassment and frustration. My adventure was turning into a fool's errand.

At the last rental car agency, I came to a counter manned by a pale, Slavic-looking fellow. I didn't bother explaining my situation since my lost luggage story had yet to elicit the sympathetic response I was hoping for. And why would it? They'd probably heard it all before from whiny, over-privileged Americans like me.

"Can you help me?" I asked.

"You're in luck," the agent said in heavily accented English. "We have one car left. It's a super-compact."

"I'll take it."

One credit-card imprint and a bunch of autographs later, I set off in search of my rental car. I laughed aloud when I saw it. It looked like a toy. It had four wheels, but it looked small enough to fit in the back of my SUV. I had thought "super-compact" was the European designation for "compact." Little did I know that it was another category down from compact, a whole other class of car. I circled the little blue Fiat 500 in disbelief, half expecting to find a wind-up key sticking out of the back. Good thing my luggage hadn't come, I thought, for I doubted it would fit. I shivered in the Irish mist, wishing I'd worn one of the sweaters I'd packed.

I went to the driver's side of the car and received yet another shock: no steering wheel. I took a closer look and saw it on the passenger side. Of course it was. In Ireland, the steering wheel was on the "wrong" side of the car, and they drove on the "wrong" side of the road. I'd known that, but hadn't given it much thought. Yet another oversight in what was rapidly becoming a long list of them. Should I get in the car? Maybe someone was trying to tell me something.

It wasn't meant to be, Barb. Listen to the signs, turn around, and go back to where you belong.

The "someone" in my head certainly wasn't Grandma Pat. I could hear her voice and see her handwriting in the frayed journals she'd left behind. In one of the early ones, she had written this: "As tall as your grandma is, she can't do your growing for you." Words to live by. Grandma Pat wouldn't want me to go back. She'd want me to press on.

Careful not to bump my head, I squeezed through the door on the right side of the car and settled in behind the wheel. Even at five-foot-three, I had to push the seat all the way back and slump my body over the steering wheel to fit inside the cramped cockpit. I adjusted the mirrors and familiarized myself with the knobs for the lights and wipers. I practiced moving my foot between the gas pedal and the brake a few times. Although the pedals were in the same configuration as in the States, they felt different when I was seated on the right instead of the left. It took a good fifteen minutes before I felt comfortable enough to start driving. I put the car into gear and crept through the parking lot.

Driving on the left side of the road was not a motor skill I had learned back home, but driving is driving—or so I thought. Without quite meaning to, I found myself on the road out of the airport. Left turns were easier than right turns, so I stayed on the left and headed toward the motorway. Relaxing a bit, I drove along for a few minutes before I somehow drifted across the centerline, ending up on the Yankee side of the road. Thankfully, there wasn't any traffic, and I swerved back into the proper lane. Soon after, I made my way to the motorway and headed south, traveling through the intensely green fields of western Ireland.

And where did I think I was going? I had no map, no itinerary. But I was going somewhere.

Just as I started to feel like I was getting the hang of my little blue Pepsi can of a car, the skies opened up and the rain came pouring down. No portentous clouds. No crack of thunder. Just a downpour of water. It was as if a giant seam in the clouds had ripped open and all the water came spilling out. I must have started hyperventilating, because soon the windows fogged up with a heavy layer of moisture, completely obscuring my vision. I had no choice but to pull over.

Maybe it was the finality of my marriage ending once and for all, the strain of knowing that my kids were worried about me, or simply the stress of travel—of so many things going so disastrously wrong. I unleashed a torrent of tears to rival the deluge outside.

What had I been thinking? My voyage of self-discovery was turning into a journey to nowhere. I hadn't familiarized myself with the towns or the roads. I had already been driving for an hour, but I had no idea where I was going. The signs looked like complete gibberish until I realized they were in Gaelic, which was about as useful. I hadn't thought to pack a raincoat, and even if I had, what good would it have done me in this mess? I cursed the airlines for losing my luggage. I cursed the sky for letting loose. But most of all, I cursed myself for so poorly planning my first real adventure.

When my tantrum ended and I stopped pounding on the steering wheel, I looked up. Not only had the rain abated, but I saw a sign I hadn't noticed when I first pulled over. It wasn't gibberish. In fact, I could read it clearly, and it listed a number of towns and their respective distances. The destination I chose wasn't the closest or the farthest, but it called out to me in a way I found impossible to resist: Dingle, 70 km.

Dingle. Not Dublin nor Donegal. Not Cork nor Kerry. Not even Westport, where my great-great-grandmother was born. I would start my adventure in Dingle.

The name made me giggle. It sounded like something out of a fairy tale—or a porno movie. The Kingdom of Dingle. The Dingle Giant. The Lucky Leprechaun and His Magic Dingle.

I would be single in Dingle. Mingle in Dingle. God knows what else I'd get up to, but I was determined to get up to it in Dingle.

—※—

Looking back, it seemed fitting that I started my exploration of Ireland on the Dingle Peninsula. I read that Saint Brendan the Navigator began his journey to North America—nearly one thousand years before Columbus—from Dingle. Brendan was an Irish monk born in 484 in the southwest of Ireland. In 530, he embarked on a journey that lasted seven years. Scholars disagree as to how far Brendan traveled, but archeologists have documented the presence of ancient Irish runes in West Virginia. Could Brendan have made it all the way across the Atlantic in his wee boat?

In the late 1970s, British adventurer Tim Severin journeyed from the Dingle Peninsula—the westernmost tip of Ireland—to North America in a handcrafted replica of Brendan's curragh, a rugged little sailing vessel. Severin successfully reenacted Saint Brendan's brave sail, but what I found most fascinating was that Saint Brendan was forty-six years old when he set sail across the Atlantic—the same age as I.

The narrow road curled around soft bends, winding between endless carpets of green. It dove, then rose again, revealing randomly scattered sheep and moss-covered rocks. Once I got the hang of driving on the wrong side of the car and the wrong side of the road, I navigated with ease. But as my fear subsided, so did my enthusiasm, and I began to feel tired and hungry. Jet lag started to kick in. The sweep of the windshield wipers across the glass and the stuffy air inside the tiny car made me sleepy. Every so often, I remembered that I still needed to buy clothes and toiletries, and my weary spirits rallied into a tizzy. I was tempted to stop for supplies in Tralee but still hadn't mastered the roundabouts.

A roundabout was basically an uncontrolled circular intersection with a central plot of grass and various roads extending like spokes on a wheel. They appeared on the outskirts of towns and villages and gave motorists the option of staying on the motorway or choosing a road toward the desired destination. Once I got the hang of navigating the circle while yielding to merging traffic, it was actually quite simple. But at first, the roundabouts were like demonic carousels—easy to get on but impossible to get off.

When I was a young girl, I recited the Irish blessing many times. It began, "May the road rise up to meet you, may the wind be always at your back." Where was the part about the blessed roundabouts and why hadn't anyone warned me about these crazy traffic circles? Even the roundabout road signs looked menacing: giant amoebas with strange names wiggling in every direction. When I finally spotted another sign for Dingle, I perked up and pushed on.

The scenery changed dramatically after Tralee. Rolling green hills gave way to villages with low stone fences that looked as if they'd been there since Saint Brendan's time. Instead of box stores and chain restaurants, I saw thatched cottages and lichened churches. Eventually, the road narrowed and I found myself in a little town bustling with men wearing wool sweaters, tweed jackets, and jaunty caps. Each one looked like the quintessential fisherman.

I nudged up the heat in my little Fiat and peered at the dash in search of the outside temperature. I found it, in Celsius, which made it feel colder than it actually was. Before I left, my friend Jean had warned me not to go to Ireland for the weather. "The only way to tell the difference between winter and summer is to measure the temperature of the rain," she had said. The perpetual moisture and cool temperatures explained the intense greenery, but it seemed surprisingly cold for summer. An old fellow with a cart pulled by a donkey waved at me as I passed.

Welcome to Dingle, I said to myself. *Now what?*

A quaint little house sat nestled among the dripping trees, surrounded by bluebells, bugles, and butterfly bushes. A sign on a wall of the house read "Bed and Breakfast." I parked the car in the gravel lot and unfolded my tortured frame from behind the wheel. The rain had stopped, and the sun had emerged from behind a bank of dark, rangy clouds. Everything smelled just as it looked—lush, fresh, clean. I, however, felt exactly the opposite, and probably smelled worse.

I pulled open the heavy door, and a rusty bell jangled, announcing my presence. The smell of freshly baked bread drifted in from the kitchen. I waited in the vestibule and looked at old, framed pictures on the wall—women with babies, men with tractors. In the next room, two wooden rocking chairs faced a large stone fireplace. I felt as if I'd stumbled into a bona fide country guesthouse, wholesome and untouched by the passage of time.

"Hallo?"

I turned to see a short, plump woman emerging from the kitchen. She wore a simple dress with lace collar and an apron around her waist. Her broad smile revealed an uneven row of yellowed teeth.

"And how might I help ya today?" She dried her hands on her apron.

"Hi. I don't have a reservation," I said, "but I'm hoping you might have a room available."

"Ah, ya're in luck, lady. We just so happen to have one for ya." The woman smoothed her apron until it was wrinkle-free.

Funny, when the news was good, I had no trouble understanding the Irish accent.

"Oh, thank you so much."

"Ya must be a Yank, then. Ya have that lovely accent." I laughed, amused to think of myself as having an accent.

"Yes, I'm from California. But you're the one with the lovely accent! If you don't mind me asking, what's your name?"

"Mrs. O'Dwyer," she said, tucking her forearms beneath her plentiful bosom.

"O'Dwyer!" I exclaimed. "That's my great-great-grandmother's name."

"Well, isn't that something?" Mrs. O'Dwyer slowly nodded her head with what seemed like mild interest and halfhearted approval.

Something good, I thought. Maybe my trip was finally on the right track. After all my setbacks and obstacles, I was being welcomed by a woman who shared my ancestor's name.

As she led me to the second floor, Mrs. O'Dwyer gave me the rundown on the inn's amenities, including meal options and tea times. Although I could only catch every other sentence or so, I listened politely to everything she said and nodded enthusiastically to feign my understanding. I couldn't help but like her. With a flourish, she opened the door of my undersized room.

"Here ya are, then. Dinner's in an hour down in the dining room. We'll see ya then."

I thanked her and inspected my room. Afternoon light filtered through the sheer, lacy curtains and rested in slanted rays on the floral comforter. Paintings of the Irish countryside hung on the rough plaster walls. With no luggage to unpack, it didn't take long for me to settle in. I would have loved a shower, but I had no clothes to change into. At the sink, I splashed some cold water on my face and freshened my makeup, but it did little to hide the bags under my eyes. I called the baggage-claim office to let them know where I was staying. Still no sign of my luggage. As I went downstairs, I made a mental note to ask Mrs. O'Dwyer where I could get some clothes to tide me over until my things turned up.

I heard the voices of my fellow boarders as I approached the dining room, and I felt a spasm of anxiety. For a minute, I considered running back to my room and burying myself under the covers. I don't know why I felt such trepidation. Normally, I wasn't a shy or timid person, but I couldn't bear another reaction like the one I'd received from the man at the baggage claim. I was alone—a single woman in a foreign land.

Of course, this wouldn't have fazed Grandma Pat, and Saint Brendan would have scoffed at my "adversity." I strutted into the room showing far more confidence than I felt.

I took a seat in an empty chair at the long wooden table and introduced myself to the other guests. To my right were British newlyweds, over the moon in love. On my left sat a French painter, a lovely older woman who had come to Ireland to capture the bucolic countryside with her brush and palette. Also at the table were a couple of girlfriends on a long weekend—a hiatus from their husbands. Seated at the head of the table was an Irishman who had come to Dingle to ride horses.

Horses? I instantly felt more comfortable. That was something I could latch onto. I could hold my own in a conversation about horses, but talk quickly changed to other subjects: local tourist attractions and, of course, the weather. I wanted to steer the discussion back to horses, but I didn't want to appear too forward or inquisitive while Mrs. O'Dwyer served up big bowls of steaming beef stew and freshly baked soda bread. The tantalizing aromas reminded me of my grandma's home cooking. I hadn't eaten since my flight, and I devoured the meal as if I might never see food again. I even splurged on a slice of chocolate potato cake. Mrs. O'Dwyer looked on with an approving smile.

After dinner, fortified by the hearty meal, I crossed the dining room and caught up with the Irishman. "Excuse me," I said. "I'd love to talk to you about horses."

The middle-aged fellow looked me over as he smoked his cigar. Crossing his arms across his broad chest, he seemed guarded, suspicious even. His weathered face and rough hands told me he knew his way around the stable.

"Back home, I used to ride almost every day," I explained. "I even had my own horse for a while."

I regretted the words as soon as I spoke them. I didn't want to revisit the painful memories of my infidelity. But hearing of our common interest seemed to put the man at ease. "Well, I'm off for an evening stroll," he said. "Join me?"

"Lead the way."

We set out together down the same road I'd taken to reach the inn. He smoked methodically, reflectively, as if he were more interested in his cigar than in speaking with me. I asked the whereabouts of the horses he intended to ride.

"Down this road a wee bit, there's a stable where ya can rent horses by the day."

"Really?" I asked, as I peered down the winding lane. My head swam with visions of sorrel steeds and black stallions, manes flying, muscles flexing. I took a deep breath and imagined the musky scent in my nostrils. I could almost feel a horse beneath me, trotting along with its rhythmic gait.

"And they let anyone rent these horses?" I asked.

"Aye," he said. "That they do."

Side by side, we walked toward the stable in the fading sunlight. The vibrant green fields along the roadside slept in the shadows of their daytime brilliance, while frogs and crickets chirped in rhythmic harmony. Coming from two entirely different worlds, the Irishman and I asked many questions of each other. He was curious about New York City and the Hoover Dam, and I wondered why the Irish drank their Guinness warm. Before we knew it, the sky began to hang like a thick purple quilt in the twilight. We headed back to the inn.

"Is all of Ireland as beautiful as this place?" I asked.

"'Tis enchanted, no doubt."

After we said our good nights, I returned to my room and flopped on the bed. Before I had a chance to undress, dreams of horses thundered through my head and sped me on my way to sleep.

Chapter 4

BLACK PUDDING AND PINTS

My first morning in Ireland greeted me with a sharp knock on the door. Startled out of a deep sleep, I struggled to make sense of the strange bed in the unfamiliar room.

"Barbara?"

"Yes?" I said, rubbing my eyes.

"Sorry to wake ya," Mrs. O'Dwyer said from outside the door, "but the baggage-claim office just called to say that they've found yar luggage. They'll deliver it here later today."

My luggage! My clothes! It all came back to me in a rush.

Ireland. Shannon. Dingle.

I thanked Mrs. O'Dwyer and forced myself out of bed. Jet lag be damned, I hadn't ventured overseas to spend the day with the covers pulled over my head. I had a wild Irish countryside to explore.

The aroma of bacon frying, bread baking—and was that beans I smelled?—lured me downstairs, where I found a weathered sideboard laden with all the provisions for a proper "fry-up." I'd eaten traditional Irish foods all my life, but nothing quite like this. I took a large plate, slid on a few fried eggs, and added a steaming scoop of hot porridge. Grandma Pat often started her day with a bowl of this Irish version of oatmeal: slow-cooked steel-cut oats with a nutty taste. I heaped my plate with bacon, sausage, and black pudding—a sinfully savory, slightly acrid concoction of offal, oats, and blood. That's right, blood, which gives it a distinctive black color. Nothing like the silky dessert we call pudding in America, but rather a kind of sausage served in half-inch-thick slices and fried in a pool of butter. Black pudding is perfect for sopping up egg yolk and, they say, cutting through hangovers. When I was a child, my grandpa used to say, "If a lassie is brave enough to eat black pudding, she'll go far in life." Well, I had tried it, even acquired a taste for it, but I hadn't gone very far in my life. Maybe Ireland would change all that.

I lingered over the morning meal, chatting with the horseman and noticing that the newlyweds missed breakfast. After everyone had gone, I poured myself another cup of tea and pulled out the postcards I had bought from Mrs. O'Dwyer. I wrote a note to each of the girls, telling them how beautiful Ireland was and that I loved and missed them. Writing my daughters made me sad. It would take time to regain their trust.

When the girls were still young, I could hear my inner critic chiding me about being a working mother when I should have been more focused on raising them. I wanted to get an *A* in my career and in motherhood, but wasn't sure I could do both. I was confused and frustrated, like a dancer having trouble learning the steps. Unsolicited, Grandma Pat had offered her two cents.

"Don't drive yourself crazy," she said one afternoon as we sat on my back-porch glider, overlooking the manicured lawn. "It's not about raising perfect children. Relax and you'll be a better mom."

"I feel like I'm not doing enough for the girls."

"Do you like your job?"

"I love helping people, but I feel like it's getting in the way."

The old vaudevillian in Grandma Pat came out. "Lighten up, Barbara," she said, giving the glider an extra push. "You have to enjoy the moment. Your kids will grow up before you know it."

I kicked off my sandals and tucked my feet beneath me, digesting Grandma Pat's words.

"Try not to be overprotective or overbearing, and remember, those girls belong to themselves. They came into this world through you, but you don't own them—they are not your property. It's your responsibility to love, care for, and nurture them. That's it. Someday, you may find yourself needing them more than they need you."

Despite Grandma Pat's advice to give my children plenty of space to grow up on their own, I abandoned my career to be a full-time mom by the time Kelly was seven and Molly twelve. Jay expedited my decision to stay home with the girls when he claimed me as his little project manager. My "job" was to take care of the kids, keep the household running, and stay home every night. The lifestyle change was bittersweet. I loved being a mom, but by leaving the workplace, I had inadvertently severed my last tie to independence. At the time, I didn't realize the importance of living a balanced life.

Upstairs, I checked to see if my luggage had magically arrived. It hadn't. Mrs. O'Dwyer had cautioned me that it could take all day for my bags to reach Dingle. I was stuck with what I had. My jeans felt as if I had worn them to cross the Atlantic by boat, but they would work for a day of riding. I went back downstairs and made the short walk to the stable.

It was a different day than the one before. The yellow, red, and green homes of Dingle popped with color against the brilliant sky, which looked vast and expansive without clouds or trees to hide it from view. Someone had turned up the green meter. The previous day's fields were a few notches brighter, freshened by the rain and shimmering in the sun.

As I walked down the lane toward the stables, I could smell the familiar scents of horses in the barn. A warm, comfortable feeling filled me when I heard their snorts, the gentle swish of their tails, and the clank of irons as stable hands flung saddles over the horses' backs. I couldn't help but think of all the days Kelly and I had spent riding together in California. Since my fling with Carson, Kelly hadn't wanted to go anywhere near the stable, let alone ride. I had taken a horseback hiatus, too. The shared passion that had brought us so close had also ripped us apart. A cold, unspoken distance hung between us. Molly was more vocal about the affair. She likened my reckless behavior to that of a runaway adolescent.

As I peeked into the livery, a young woman greeted me. Her simple braid, classic English riding pants, cable sweater, and tall leather boots embodied the equestrian lifestyle I'd fallen in love with as a girl. I envied the flush in her cheeks and the pureness of youth that shone in her face—ruddy, windblown, and vibrant.

"Might I help ya, miss?"

"I want to rent a horse for the day. Can I do that here?"

"So ya can." She held out her hand. "Name's Fiona, Fiona O'Ryan, and I run the place. And if ya decide to ride, I'll be yer guide. Have a look at me stock, then?"

Fiona led me to the corral where she kept her horses for hire, all different colors and sizes. I chose a bay Connemara, a breed known for its athleticism and good temperament, qualities that made it an excellent mount for children and tentative tourists. I'd never ridden an authentic Irish horse before and was excited at the prospect.

"How'd you like to go for a ride, girl?" I asked the horse. "I'll bet you can keep me on the right side of the road."

The mare tossed her black mane and sneezed at me, which I took as a yes. I ran a hand down her soft nose. She had fine features but was solid through her chest and loins.

"What's her name?"

"'We call her Mud in Yer Eye. I think the two of ya will be just grand together."

I couldn't wait to ride in Ireland, but somehow it didn't seem right without Kelly. I missed my little girl. I pictured us together outside the stable back home, grooming our horses and chatting about everything and nothing. Kelly's zest for riding had reconnected me to the powerful energy of horses and brought us closer together. When we were out for the day, a picnic in the orange groves became part of our ritual. We'd stare at the afternoon sky and talk about our day. At the end of our rides, we washed the sweat off the glistening horses with water from the hose, often spraying each other in the process. Afterward, we combed the horses' manes, cleaned their hooves, and fed them. It was meditative, almost Zen-like.

After that fateful night in Paso Robles, Kelly associated horses with my disastrous affair, and I wasn't sure if she would ever ride again. I was still passionate about horses, and I wanted her to be, too—just like the old days. Even though Molly didn't ride, she was on my mind, too. She was getting ready to start her sophomore year at college. Molly was at a turning point in her life, a time when she needed to start making decisions about her career path and her future. I wanted to be there for her, to help her evaluate her options, but she didn't want me. I'd hoped this trip would give my girls the space they needed to take the next step as young women, but instead I felt as if I'd abandoned them.

I hadn't come to Ireland, though, to beat myself up over my past. I came to forge new memories, ones that someday I could share with my girls. The only way to do that was to make my experiences memorable. I mounted my horse and let out a loud "Yee-haw."

Fiona laughed. She effortlessly jumped on her steed and beckoned me to follow her.

"Quite excited, eh?" She squeezed her horse's sides with her thighs, and he moved forward.

"I'm sorry," I said as our horses walked through the gate and onto the road. "I didn't realize how much I'd missed riding. It's been a while."

Fiona winked at me. "Well, just do what ya feel."

As we rode, Fiona pointed out the harbor in the distance, where Fungi the Dingle Dolphin, a solitary bottlenose, welcomed fisherman and tourists into Dingle Bay. Sailboats and kayaks skimmed the shoreline, and sharp cliffs met the water in a dramatic seam. Fiona's family had lived in the region for generations, so she explained all the mysteries and secrets a passerby might miss. She talked at a slow pace and told me just enough to leave me curious for more. I enjoyed her cadence.

We rode along a small cobblestone lane through fields of peat and pastures flecked with heather. She pointed out rocks with Gaelic writing and barely discernable pathways that had preceded modern roads. When we came to an old stone structure, Fiona dismounted.

"Come on," she said. "Follow me."

I hopped off my horse, tied her up to the fence that lined the lane, and followed Fiona into the triangular building. I had to crouch down and practically crawl through the door, but once inside, I stood up and took in my surroundings. Dry-stacked stones formed the sloping walls. A single window let a beam of sunlight into the cool interior.

"It seems old," I said.

"'Tis. Over a thousand years old," Fiona said. "The Gallarus Oratory, one of the most famous landmarks in all of Dingle. Built without mortar of any kind."

I ran my hands over the stones stacked from floor to ceiling where the walls met in an arch.

"Can ya imagine the skill it took to do that? Even after all this time, it remains intact and completely watertight."

I admired the building's craftsmanship. A small ancient place, humble but beautiful. A place of deep quiet, an old quiet, as if no one had spoken in there for hundreds of years. It seemed strange that so many castles had tumbled to the ground or fallen into ruin, but that pile of rocks remained standing, even without any "glue" to hold it together.

"There's a legend that says if ya leave through this window, yer soul will be cleansed," Fiona said. I looked skeptically at the tiny hole in the stone wall. It seemed like a worthy cause, but I only got about halfway through.

"I'm stuck!" I called to Fiona. "Does this means only my heart was cleansed? What about the rest of me?"

Fiona laughed. "I could probably push ya through, but ya would go straight to heaven, because ya would die in the process."

I backed my way out of the window and exited the way I came in.

Fiona and I got back on our horses and continued our ride, exploring more ancient monuments and the remnants of crumbling walls built to protect the borough. Fiona pointed up at the hillside.

"See those?"

All I could see were rocks. I kept staring until a pattern emerged in the distance.

"Those are called fairy forts. The remains of circular dwellings built by the Celts way back in the Iron Age. Legend has it that bad luck will befall anyone who demolishes the forts or the surrounding land."

There lay my ancient history. But was it really history if I could see it with my eyes, touch it with my hands? Ireland's rich tradition of fairies and myths made sense in a place where past and present coincided.

We rode up one hill and down another, gently swaying from side to side as the horses picked their way through the fields. Exploring Dingle on horseback offered the perfect pace for that ancient land. Each step took me further back in time, as if the land itself had opened up and taken me into another world. It was easy to imagine the fields like they were thousands of years ago. Not like the California I knew, where there was always a freeway in the distance, electrical wires in the sky, or an SUV rushing down the road. In Ireland, I could imagine that the last thousand years simply hadn't happened. I felt as if I were exactly where I was supposed to be.

When we came upon a white sandy beach, Mud in Yer Eye seemed to sense her opportunity to cut loose. It took everything I had to hold her back.

"Just keep yer feet in the stirrups and enjoy the ride," Fiona yelled.

I took her advice. We launched off at a full gallop along the water's edge and flew down the beach, our manes flowing in the wind. I looked over my shoulder at Fiona, who had one arm raised to shield her eyes from the flying sand. The meaning of my horse's name was instantly evident. As the horses kicked up wet clumps of sand and pounded through the waves, an orchestra that followed my horse's rhythm began to play in my mind. It blocked out all other sounds, as if a hush descended on the landscape—all of nature listening to our symphony of surf and sand. I didn't feel like a woman riding a horse on the beach. It was as if the horse, the sand, the sea, and I were all one creature. Soaked from head to toe, I felt as if I'd been baptized.

We didn't stop until we hit the end of the three-mile stretch. The horses gleamed with sweat. I was breathing heavily and felt as if I hadn't flexed my riding muscles in a long time. When I saw Fiona wipe her brow, I felt better. We were both exhausted from the ride. My stomach growled loud enough for Fiona to hear it, so we stopped for lunch at a neighborhood pub. We tied our horses outside, which reinforced my sense of having stepped back in time. I half-expected a buggy to roll down the cobblestone road.

"Is it safe to leave our horses here?" I asked.

Fiona let out a full-throated guffaw. "Not a lot of horse-jackers around here!"

I had to laugh as well. I never dreamed of leaving something so valuable unattended and out in the open without some sort of antitheft device attached to it. I was used to living in a world where everything I possessed was gated, guarded, or locked down. Myself included.

I stretched my calves and alternately shook each leg. My muscles were a quivering mess from being on the horse for so long. I stumbled inside the pub and practically staggered to the bar. I ordered a pint of Guinness and, at Fiona's suggestion, Dingle pie—a pastry filled with mutton and served with a jug of broth to pour over it. As we talked, Fiona suggested possible routes we could take for the afternoon and described some of the sights she thought I should see. I told her I wanted to do and see it all. I sipped the velvety stout while I waited for my food. When it arrived, I devoured the pie and ordered another pint to wash it down.

"I'm not in any hurry," I said, scooping up the last scrap of pastry soaked with broth.

"That's good," she said. "You'll find 'hurry' doesn't mean much in the west of Ireland."

After lunch, we rode to an area where Fiona told me horses used to run unbridled and free. The open spaces were rich and lush, carpeted in emerald green. We passed an old fort, a stone farmhouse, an outcropping of slate-like gray rocks. Here and there, flocks of fluffy white sheep watched us as we passed. As we rode on, the hills became a darker green, with dirt roads carving out the local routes into town. We crested a hill and our view sprawled into a maze of farmland—neatly divided into plots with low, rock-wall boundaries where farmers had worked the land for centuries. I imagined what it would be like to wake up in such an idyllic place every day. It must have been hard for my ancestors to leave that land.

We traveled back over the mossy knolls and valleys, my horse and I moving as one at an easy gait. Though my body ached from riding all day, my spirit was alive and humming.

Back at the stable, Fiona and I put up the horses. When everything was finished, we walked down the road to another pub, alive with music. We knocked back several pints, each one sweeter than the last. We listened to the music, brisk and lilting beneath the low ceiling. The fiddler reminded me of Grandpa Harold, who never went to school past the third grade but knew hundreds of songs from his own parents' vaudeville theater shows. After every night's raucous show, the troupe went back to my great-grandparents' house for a midnight feast of pot roast, potatoes, and cabbage. I recalled Grandpa Harold's zest and humor.

"Being Irish is very much a part of who I am," he used to say. "I take it everywhere with me."

I'd laugh, and he'd roll off another.

"A good laugh and a long sleep are the two best cures for anything."

I especially liked that one.

My grandfather dressed like someone in an old black-and-white movie. He often wore a top hat and flourished a cane like a dandy. He was a great match for Grandma Pat. When they came to visit, they'd teach me the steps to ballroom dancing, twirling and laughing all night long. The next morning, we'd walk to the corner store where Grandpa Harold taught me to reach out my hand, look the neighbors in the eye, and introduce myself. It was a lesson I never forgot.

While I watched the fiddler, an animated Irishman with a mass of black curls slipped past Fiona and sidled up to me. I followed Grandpa's advice and introduced myself.

"Shane," he countered. "Ya're a new one in these parts." He held out his hand to lead me onto the dance floor. "C'mere and we'll have a dance."

I hesitated, embarrassed about getting up in front of the local crowd, but Fiona urged me on. Irish dancing with Shane was nothing like ballroom dancing with my grandparents—and people were watching. What if I did something wrong?

"Jist smile and bend yer knees," Shane instructed.

I looked down at my knees and did as I was told. "Like this?"

"Exactly!" he said. "Now, lift yer feet, while keeping yer knees bent."

"How am I doing?" I looked around, trying to mimic the other dancers.

"Ya're a natural!"

It really was just that easy. No shimmying from side to side, no jumping around. The Irish danced from the hip down, so while their legs were flying around, their torsos remained as stiff as a tailor's dummy. I remembered hearing that they adopted this tradition so they could dance behind a low wall without the Brits knowing what they were up to. Before I knew it, I was dancing right along with everyone else. With no need to hide behind walls, I locked arms with my partner and bobbed up and down to the rhythm of the music. I tapped my toes, jerked my knees, and whirled about in magical confusion. My grandparents had taught me well!

At the end of the set, Shane led me straight to the bar.

"Yer heart may be pure, Barbara, but the devil has a hold of ya below the waist!"

Ain't that the truth, I thought, reflecting on the complicated path that had led to me Ireland.

Chapter 5

FINDING MY RELIGION

The previous day's ride and late-night jig nearly did my legs in. They practically screamed as I hobbled around my room in Mrs. O'Dwyer's B&B. But as bad as my legs felt, my head hurt a little bit more. Okay, a lot more. I wasn't accustomed to drinking so much alcohol. The dark Guinness had flowed into my pint glass in black waves, and I'd been all-too-eager to surf atop its creamy froth.

Still, nothing would keep me from another day of riding, and I made my way to Fiona's stable. A gentle rain had left the turf spongy—perfect for my sore head and tired legs. The Irish had an expression for it: "soft." The sky was soft, the air was soft, the meadows were soft, as were the cows. And anyone who'd seen me that morning would have thought I was soft in the head. I willed away my headache and set off skipping, twirling down the road, my smile as broad as the River Shannon. That's how happy I was to be in the town of Dingle in County Kerry in the southwest of Ireland.

Then I heard it. An obnoxious, jarring sound—the opposite of soft. It was Sunday morning, and clanging bells restored the pain in my head. While my upbringing was typical of most Irish-American girls, one aspect definitely was not: I didn't grow up Catholic. Rather, I was raised as the daughter of Christian fundamentalists. Our Baptist church was one of fire and brimstone, hellfire and fury, with strict rules and even stricter punishments. My family attended church every Sunday, no exceptions. I sang in the church choir and joined the youth group. Instead of trips to amusement parks during spring and summer breaks, I went to vacation Bible school and overnight revival camps. I even went on international missionary trips. My parents were proud of my involvement in these devout activities and happily financed them. They figured it was a good investment in my path to heaven.

Our church was at odds with my ancestors' Catholicism and Grandma Pat's interest in Eastern religions. From an early age, I understood how our church's beliefs seemed out of step with the rest of California. Tolerance for others and freedom to be yourself weren't ideas discussed in our church—or at home. If my father had seen me drinking and dancing at the pub in the Irish countryside, he would have tensed up and shaken his head, probably feeling like a failure as a parent. Imagine what he thought about my divorce.

The church bells did not bring to mind bucolic scenes of a community coming together, but scenes of stinging shame and harsh recriminations for those who stepped out of line. I put my head down and quickened my pace to Fiona's stable. The sun was beginning to penetrate the thin gray clouds and held the promise of a beautiful day. Hangover or no hangover, I was determined to make the most of it. But first, I wanted to get as far away from those church bells as possible.

"How ya feeling this morning?" Fiona asked when I reached the barn. Dressed in crisp riding trousers and a hunter-green jacket, she looked as vibrant as she had the day before.

"I haven't had that much fun in a long time!" I answered.

"Ya seemed a wee bit knackered."

The sun peeked through the clouds, and I squinted at her through the sunlight that bathed the morning in brightness. "I'm out of practice. How is it you look so awake, and I can barely open my eyes?"

"Ah, all in a day's work for an Irish lass," she said with a wink. "I was wondering if ya might want to ride over to a church service this morning?"

My heart sank. Church? I didn't have the heart to let Fiona down. I'd told her about my Irish roots. She probably assumed I was Catholic.

"I'd love to," I lied. "Let's go." I hoped it was Fiona's idea of a joke, a kind of penance for the previous night's merrymaking. I'd been counting on a long, leisurely ride in the grassy foothills, not a hurried trot to a stuffy service.

Neither of us spoke as we rode. The chirping of the birds, the distant cowbells, and the crackling of branches and leaves beneath the horses' hooves were like sacred music in the stillness. I heard the church bells again and realized we were heading away from town, not toward it. In every village I'd passed through, the church was in the center of town, mirroring its role in the community. Why were we riding into the countryside?

"Here we are." Fiona reined to a stop. "We're near Slea Head. If you look out, you can see the Blasket Islands," she said, dismounting. She tied her horse to a tree, then grabbed the blanket she had lashed to the back of her saddle.

I stayed on my horse for a few minutes longer, taking in the view from the western tip of the Dingle Peninsula. With the sun at my back, I felt the brisk breeze coming up off the water. The hills rolled out like a welcoming carpet, but along the shoreline, they changed their attitude and dropped to the sea in threatening cliffs. From my vantage point, the flat water cradled the islands before disappearing beyond the horizon. Ahead of its frothy wake, a small ferry chugged toward the largest island.

I took a deep gulp of air and breathed out a "wow" before I dismounted and tied my horse next to Fiona's. I tried to rearrange my jacket and hair, certain I would make a spectacle of myself by arriving at church in riding gear.

Fiona led me to a gently sloping hill with a bowl at its bottom, a natural amphitheater. Villagers clad in subtle scarves, felt caps, and faded jackets sat on the ground, clustered in small groups. I'd been concerned about the way we were dressed, but we fit right in. People chatted with each other brightly, and I heard occasional laughter.

"What religion is this?" I asked. I couldn't quite figure out if these people were worshipping or having a picnic—they were so relaxed and actually seemed to be having fun.

"Celtic Christianity," Fiona said, pronouncing "Celtic" with a hard *c* as in cat.

"I've never heard of that," I said. It seemed worlds away from the strict Baptist religion I was raised on. "Are there rules for joining this church?"

"Nary a one," Fiona said as she started down the slope.

"So what do you believe?" I asked, curious about her religious beliefs. I was probably twice her age, but after the year I'd been through I was no longer sure what I believed—or didn't believe.

"I have a hard time defining 'God,'" she said. "It seems like an empty attempt to put wee boundaries on something infinite. I feel the divine everywhere, but especially in nature—Mother Nature—that's what drew me to Celtic Christianity. Here in Ireland, Celtic religious beliefs existed long before Christianity. People live in harmony with nature, balancing the physical and the spiritual. What ya see here is a blending of the two."

Fiona spread the fringed plaid blanket and kept talking as we sat down.

"Celts are fiercely independent folks. They have a deep passion for freedom and a profound reverence for nature. That's what got us in trouble—people from organized religions. They didn't understand us. Instead, they bungled things up by misinterpreting our beliefs, and we were cast as pagans, country folk, people of the land." Fiona tucked a stray strand of hair behind her ear to keep it from blowing in the wind. "We don't worship nature but rather God *in* nature. We strive to be true to ourselves, not to a religion that tells us who we should be."

"Fiona, you're a heathen!" I said, laughing. I was comfortable enough with her to know that she wouldn't take this as an insult. The people who raised me would call her a heretic and nonbeliever, just because she risked being herself.

A discordant fiddle opened the service. The player stood alone in the center of the amphitheater, his music magnified by the natural acoustics. He wore a lightweight cable sweater and a pair of dark trousers, and he cocked his head to one side to hold his instrument in place.

"It sounds so ... old," I whispered.

"'Tis," she replied. "The fiddle tune ya're hearing is an ancient hymn."

When he was finished, a large gray-haired woman took his place on the flat, grassy stage and sang a haunting song in Gaelic. Though I couldn't make out the words, I could tell it was a tale full of sadness.

"She's singing a song about Mary," Fiona said. "Fair, gentle Mary."

Okay, maybe I was wrong about the sadness. Nonetheless, the air felt sacred, accompanied by a powerful feeling of peace. Everything seemed connected, and I was a part of it. I tried to hold on to the feeling, to take what was good and meaningful and make it my own.

The Celtic ceremony could not have been more different from the Sunday services I attended as a child. There was no central figure, no domineering preacher standing over the masses, delivering a reprimanding sermon from the pulpit. In my church, religion and ritual went hand in hand. Here the service came from the congregants. Poetry here, singing there, and music wafting through the trees.

After the hour-long service, Fiona and I each took one end of the blanket and neatly folded it before walking back up the slope to our horses.

"What did ya think?" Fiona asked.

"It was very ... different." I was at a loss for words.

"How so?"

"I don't know." I tried to explain how, for the first time, it felt like

God was meeting me, instead of me approaching him. I stumbled over my sentences. "I probably sound like a blundering fool."

"It's not that complicated," Fiona replied. "Like I said before, sometimes we try to define the indefinable, and we call the mess that we make of it 'God.' But it's not about how ya define things, it's what ya believe."

I nodded. I liked that there were finally no rules governing my thoughts and actions. And I liked that a sharp young woman could help guide me to a deeper understanding. While the morning service didn't leave me with a burning desire to convert to Celtic Christianity, it did show me that it was possible to draw bits and pieces from different beliefs to form my own kind of religion—much as Grandma Pat had done. It was a new approach to spirituality, and I felt lightheaded at the prospect of having a relationship with the God of my own choosing.

Something had awakened inside me. Maybe it was faith. Maybe it was God. A melody, a rhythm, a beat. Grandma Pat had heard it, and she danced to it every day of her life. I didn't know what to do with the music inside me, but I didn't want to die with it locked away inside. Unlistened to. Unheard. I had to find a way to let it out.

Chapter 6

WITCHES AND SAINTS

Fiona and I returned our horses to the stable, then went into town together. With a population of just over a thousand, Dingle was small enough to explore on foot. We paused at windows displaying intricate jewelry shaped into Celtic symbols, large earthenware urns glazed with lustrous finishes, and handwoven scarves in classic plaids and soft heathers. Fiona led me to a tiny bookstore, and I lost a few hours thumbing through volumes about Celtic Christian practices. I wasn't ready to convert after attending the hillside service, but the titles tugged at me and piqued my interest. As I browsed the shelves, I thought of Grandma Pat's journals with her notes on religions from around the world.

That's when I spotted a collection of books that described Wicca, the practice of modern witchcraft. Was Wicca part of Celtic Christianity? Did Fiona leave that part out when we went to the service for fear of scaring me off? Or had I stumbled upon something entirely different?

Curious, I picked up a thin paperback and skimmed through it. It gave a bit of history, then moved into contemporary practice. It didn't come off as fiction. I was pretty sure it was the real deal, but the whole concept was just too weird for me. Sorcery? Spells? Spirits? I shoved the book back on the shelf and abruptly left the bookstore. My life was complicated enough already. I didn't need any Irish voodoo.

Fiona followed me as I left. "Everything all right?" she asked.

"Everything is great," I said. "There's just so much to see." I hoped this would explain my hasty departure.

We walked down Dingle's narrow lanes, passing bakeries with pastries and pies, more gift shops, and corner markets. Each storefront was coated in a thick layer of paint—deep maroon, slate blue, sage green—and accented by contrasting molding. A few stone structures nestled between the walls of color. It looked like a postcard, where every third business was a pub.

I considered myself open to new experiences, but upon reflection, my reaction to the books on Wicca was that of a conservative, closed-minded person. *Great,* I thought. I'd traveled five thousand miles to confirm that I'd become my mother, set in her ways and devoted to her religion. I once saw a Buddhist monk when I was a child. Mom told me that Buddhism was a cult. But then, anything besides Christianity was part of the devil's cult in my parents' eyes.

To prove that I wasn't a younger, more fashionably dressed version of my mom, I took Fiona into a small shop with tarot cards and beaded wands in the storefront window. Inside, the spicy scent of burning incense tickled my nose and soft Celtic music soothed my ears. A rack in the center of the room displayed long, hooded robes.

"I love this shop," Fiona said as we browsed the shelves near the front door. "In fact, I know someone who works here." She looked around for her friend.

Behind the counter stood a willowy woman who looked like a Druid priestess. She had porcelain skin and hazel eyes. Flaming red hair draped her shoulders, and she wore an outfit I imagined someone might wear to a Renaissance festival. Gaudy rings festooned her hands.

"This is Bridget," Fiona said. "She's a witch."

It took everything in my power not to ask, "Are you a good witch or a bad witch?" like Dorothy in *The Wizard of Oz.*

"Hello," I said with a quaver in my voice.

"Don't be frightened," Bridget said.

"I'm sorry. I don't mean to seem rude, but when I think of witches, I just think of ..."

"I know, flying hags and devil worship. Tell me this. When ya think of wizards, what images do ya conjure up?"

Fiona stood off to the side, listening to our exchange, a soft smile on her face.

"Well, wizards seem more magical, granting wishes instead of casting spells," I said. "I never thought of it before, but it seems like I perceive mystical females as bad and their male counterparts as good."

Bridget chuckled. Her appearance enchanted me, but it took some concentration to adjust to her brogue. Every time I met someone new, I felt as if I were learning a new language. But Bridget had a musical voice and a gentle laugh that I enjoyed, and she seemed eager to talk.

"People typically think of witches as stirring up potions in big cauldrons and practicing black magic. In olden times, before Christianity, witches were midwives and healers. We commanded great respect within the community by healing with compassion, from the heart."

"I had no idea. This is all so new to me."

"Some folks are more comfortable with the term 'Wiccan' than 'witch,'" Bridget said. "Wiccans live by one credo: if it harms no one, do as ya will, for what ya do returns threefold. It's like this," she continued. "White magic means to wish positive thoughts on someone. Black magic is just the opposite. We believe that what ya put out is what ya receive in return. We do not wish negative thoughts on anyone or anything, for nature and the universe are one."

I reflected on my own Christianity. It wasn't so different. The Bible said, "A man reaps what he sows," and, "Do unto others as you would have them do unto you."

"Women have been a healing force since the beginning of time. Wiccans celebrate our femininity and its power. We bleed, give birth, tend the soul. We're the collective mother of the land."

"Wiccans or women?"

"Both!" Bridget said. "Unfortunately, men were threatened by this power, so they burned Wiccans at the stake, thinking they could get rid of them. But they couldn't do it. Wiccans returned, time and time again. We're still here today. Ah, but listen to me go on. What is it ya're seeking?"

"I'm not sure," I said. I had no idea what I was doing there, in that shop, talking to a witch. I knew that I wanted to break the cycle of being close-minded like my mother, and I knew that I wanted to give my daughters an example of how to live openly with a curiosity to learn. But those were loose desires. I needed something more concrete.

"So ya're on a journey to find yerself?" Bridget asked.

I nodded, suddenly overcome with emotion. I felt the heat of embarrassment in my cheeks as my eyes became wet, and I blinked away the tears. I was a sophisticated, educated woman, not some patchouli-wearing crystal gazer looking for answers in mystical realms because the world was such a disappointment. Or was I?

Maybe that's what I'd become. A disappointed wife. A disappointing mother and daughter. A disappointment, not only to others, but also to myself. Standing in a wacky witchcraft shop in a foreign country, I realized that perhaps I hadn't lived up to what I could have been. I wanted to be more.

"That ya're even on the path means ya're halfway through the journey. Real faith is found in the search for God."

I thought of Albert Einstein's quote, "I want to know God's thoughts. The rest are details." He searched through science. I was looking elsewhere.

A couple of tourists came in, noticed that we were deep in conversation, and quickly left after a cursory glance around the shop. While Bridget and I talked, Fiona waited, occasionally picking up a pointed pendulum or smelling a scented candle.

"I feel a little lost," I said. "I'm searching for answers by trying to discover what I really believe, but I'm not sure I even know the questions."

"Ah, child, ya already have the answers—right here," she said, pressing her palm to my chest. I felt like she was reading my heart.

Bridget suggested I visit a well dedicated to her namesake, and she wrote out the directions to Liscannor, about three hours north of Dingle. It seemed like an important step in my journey, so I thanked Bridget and left the shop with Fiona.

I didn't buy anything at the shop, nor did I leave empty-handed. I felt as if I'd been given a gift, a cherished souvenir I'd long since given up hope of ever finding. Bridget had affirmed that I'd planted the seed of self-discovery. I was going to nourish that little sprout until it grew into a strong and independent me—a woman I could be proud of, not disappointed in.

As we walked back through the town, Fiona was quiet, politely allowing me time to digest my Wiccan experience. After a few minutes, I asked her if she believed in modern witchcraft.

"I believe there is power in being a woman," she said. "I try not to get too caught up in putting people and their beliefs in boxes."

"That's a great attitude to have," I said. "I've spent over forty years living in black and white. Gray areas never existed for me, and now I'm finding them to be the most colorful aspects of life." Fiona smiled. "And what about Saint Brigid?" I asked. "I understand that she was the founder of women's religious life in Ireland, but I'm confused about a lot of things. Was she a pagan goddess or Catholic saint?"

"Everyone seems to have a different story," Fiona said. "I like to think of her as a mystical, magical symbol of feminine spirituality."

I thanked Fiona for showing me the town, and we parted ways. My night of drinking and dancing had finally caught up with me, and I headed back to the B&B. Before I went up to my room, Mrs. O'Dwyer asked me about my day. Instead of telling her I'd been hanging out with witches all day, I asked her what she knew about Saint Brigid.

For Mrs. O'Dwyer, Brigid was the patron saint of women, wanderers, and children born out of wedlock. When I looked up Saint Brigid on the Internet, I became even more confused. Why were there so many variations in the spelling of her name? Was it Bridget, Brigid, Brigit, Bride, or Brid? Were they even the same person or a multitude of historical women all lumped together? There didn't seem to be much agreement as to when or where she lived. There were towns, churches, and shrines devoted to her all over Ireland. She was all things to all people—in Ireland anyway.

I said my good-byes to the folks I'd met in Dingle, packed up my little Fiat, and went in search of Saint Brigid's Well. As I passed back through Tralee and continued north toward Tarbert, I confidently spun through the roundabouts. It was just a matter of practice, and I had mastered the technique. Each of the towns I passed was wrapped in a low stone wall that followed the winding road. The stones, strewn with tufts of grass, looked as if they had been there since the beginning of time.

After I had been on the road for an hour or so, a herd of sheep stopped my progress. A man and a girl were guiding their flock across the road. When the man reached the other side, he turned to wait for the girl, who had stopped to pick a flower from the roadside. His patience touched me. My father never slowed down for anyone, especially his own children. He used to drag us around, never waiting for me or my sisters to catch up. There was no time for questions or room to explore a different way of doing things. His way was the right way and the only way. But in Ireland, observing the man and the girl move the flock forward, I realized that there was more than one right way.

I meandered along the twisty roads—I had yet to see a straight road in that country. I arrived in Tarbert ahead of the scheduled ferry that would take my Fiat and me across the finger of water that divided County Kerry from County Clare, so I stopped for a pint. Nursing my drink, I stood at the bar to stretch my legs, cramped from the long hours in my tiny car. Pubs in Ireland were like convenience stores in the States: one on every corner. More than just a place to get a drink, Irish pubs were public meeting places where townsfolk gathered to eat and socialize.

By the time I finished my pint, it was nearly time for the ferry. I drove to the landing and boarded with a handful of other vehicles, all of them bigger than mine. We crossed the Shannon Estuary on a rumbling old vessel that smelled of diesel and mildew, but I still thought it was romantic.

The afternoon gave way to evening, and a full moon appeared from behind a stand of trees. By the time I arrived at Saint Brigid's Well, the sun had set and the moonlight cast soft shadows behind the headstones of a hilltop cemetery overlooking the bay. It was an eerie spot to find myself alone. I parked the car and checked the glove box in hopes of finding a flashlight but didn't come across one.

I got out of the car, pulled a wool sweater over my head, and followed the signs to the well. The moon lit up the gravel pathway, but I still felt spooked by my surroundings. Looking over my shoulder, I considered driving into Liscannor proper to find a room for the night. The well would still be there in the morning.

"Welcome to Saint Brigid's Well," called a voice from the darkness. "Are ya Barbara?"

I whipped my head around and clutched my handbag to my chest. A woman came toward me, wearing a hooded robe that looked like those I had seen in at the shop in Dingle. She was tall and thin, much like Bridget, but it was too dark for me to see her face. Her hair was tucked beneath the hood, draped loosely over her head.

"How did you know?" I asked, utterly dumbstruck.

"We Wiccans stick together, and Bridget is a good friend of mine. She called to tell me ya were coming this way, and mentioned that ya might be late in getting here. I offered to meet ya, give ya a bit of a personal tour. Call me Naidra."

"Such a pretty name."

"Thanks very much. It means 'small spring.'"

She extended her right hand, and I debated whether I should shake it, when I saw that she was handing me a candle. I was beginning to think Ireland was full of witches. Apparently, when Saint Patrick tried to rid the island of pagans, he'd missed a few.

"Thanks!" I said, taking the candle. Before she withdrew her hand, I noticed that she had an extra finger on her hand, and I almost jumped.

"Come this way," she said, waving at me with her irregular hand. "I'll show ya where the well is." At that point, I wondered if I might be dreaming, if I would wake up and find myself back in my bed in California, wondering what Ireland would be like.

I shivered, and I would be lying if I said it was just from the chill in the air. To be perfectly honest, the place gave me the creeps, but at the same time, it intrigued me. I followed the woman through the tilting tombstones, strangely beautiful in their crumbling state. Walking through a moonlit cemetery with a stranger, I felt a peculiar sense of comfort, as if it were nothing out of the ordinary to go traipsing through a graveyard with a woman in a hooded robe, waving her six-fingered hand. In the movies, scenes like that always ended badly, but I wasn't afraid—at least that's what I told myself.

To cover up my anxiety, I brought up Saint Brigid, confessing my confusion. Naidra told me that places associated with Brigid were considered sacred long before Christianity came to Ireland.

"In Celtic tradition," she explained, "one of the most powerful priestesses was a goddess named Brigid. Saint Brigid was probably named after the goddess as a way to Christianize her." We picked our way among the tombstones, using our candles to light up the shadows. "Today, the Irish pay homage to Saint Brigid by placing her cross over their doorways to protect their homes."

I had seen those crosses in Dingle, prominently hanging inside of shops and homes around town. There was even one at the stable. The humble cross, crafted from dried rushes, looked a bit like a pinwheel. The middle was a woven square, with each arm tied off at the end.

As we strolled among the tombstones, I saw signs of new life erupting, shoots of grass around the monuments of death. To me, they were symbols of hope and vitality. They had healing power, not because they had medicinal properties, but because I believed in them. In a way, these burgeoning seedlings were like faith, yielding power to those who believed. But faith is a personal experience, with different rewards and consequences for everyone.

"Are you interested in Wicca?" Naidra asked, as we descended moss-covered stone steps from the cemetery toward a lower area.

"I'm interested in the healing aspects," I said. "I'm trained as a physical therapist."

"That's wonderful. Wiccans—like all women—have different strengths and powers. While I focus on spirituality, healing is what interests me most, much like it does you. I have a feeling that you will use this more as you go forward in your own journey."

Use what more? I wanted to ask, but we'd reached our destination. We paused to pass through a creaking gate, then stepped inside an iron fence. Not for the first time was I grateful for the brightness of the moon.

"Is that the well?" I asked, peering inside a little stone structure that covered a dark hole in the ground.

"We Irish call this a spring." Her voice was low and throaty, but I could hear the kindness in it. "Springs hold very special meaning for us. A spring breaking through the hard earth symbolizes the freshness that can suddenly dawn within a heart that remains open. There are over three thousand springs in Ireland. Dozens are named for Saint Brigid," she said, slipping her deformed hand inside the wide sleeve of her robe. It seemed like a well-practiced habit.

"Why so many?"

"Saint Brigid represents the flame of creativity and inspiration. Whether we call her a saint or a goddess, she is within us all, giving us the passion to believe in ourselves with conviction."

The Wiccan's words had a strange effect on me. They felt as if they were specifically for me. They were more than words, but answers—the notions I had come to Ireland to investigate. Then again, all travelers who sought the wisdom from the wells probably felt the same way. Nevertheless, I felt relaxed. Safe.

"What's down there?" I asked. It wasn't a very spiritual question, but my curiosity got the best of me.

"In the past, springs were seen as a threshold between the dark, unknown, subterranean world and the outer world of light and form. Springs were revered as special apertures through which divinity flowed. And when a spring awakens in the mind, new possibilities begin to flow."

"Like a wishing well?"

She nodded and went through the arched doorway. "Come," she said.

I joined her and held up my candle to get a better view. Trinkets and treasures were piled high in shocking disarray. Photos of Jesus, carvings of the Virgin Mary draped in rosary beads, and burned-out votive candles covered every square inch inside the stone shelter.

Naidra knelt down at the edge of the well, which was rimmed with stone, and motioned for me to do the same. "First, you must drink from the spring three times," she said.

A chipped earthen mug sat on the well's rim. She filled it with cool water and offered it to me. I took three tentative sips. The water tasted fresh and pure. Holy.

I watched as Naidra withdrew a satin ribbon from inside her robe and fingered it gently with all six of her digits. I must have looked alarmed or even mesmerized, for she smiled.

"Yes, I do have an extra finger. It came with the package. Seems rather mystical, doesn't it?"

She'd caught me staring. "You don't see that every day," I said.

"I suppose it's a good thing I wasn't born a hundred years ago or I'd have been burned at the stake."

"What's the ribbon for?"

"People come here from all over to make their deepest, most fervent desires known. If ya were to come here during the day, ya would see folks, old and young, asking Saint Brigid to make their hopes and dreams come true." I could smell her musky perfume as she spoke.

"Does it really work?" I asked. I hadn't planned on going there, much less having wishes granted by an ancient saint.

"Any ritual is hollow and meaningless if ya just go through the motions. For it to work, ya have to believe. If ya don't, it's a waste of time."

She closed her eyes as she fingered the ribbon and whispered a few words to herself. Then, holding the ribbon over the mouth of the well, she released it. She withdrew another ribbon from her cloak and handed it to me.

"Yer turn," she said.

I took the satiny bit of material and closed my eyes. After a few moments of reflection, longing to believe, I opened my eyes and dropped the ribbon down the dark hole. I smiled as it disappeared into the depths. Could something as simple as a hole in the ground really have such transforming power? Could a ribbon and a spring help me find myself? Would this ritual join the gaping rifts between me and the women I loved—my mother, my sisters, and my daughters?

We stepped outside the little building and walked back through the gate to a large oak tree near a gurgling brook fed by the holy spring. Its branches were adorned with a colorful assortment of rags and rolled-up bits of paper.

"What's this? More wishes?"

"Aye, these are spiritual messages from travelers like yerself."

At the base of the tree were lit votive candles, photographs, and other beloved mementos left behind by those who had passed through. Naidra drew out a small notebook from the folds of her robe and handed it to me. A gust of wind ruffled the pages of the notebook and made her robe flap loudly as it blew around her legs.

"Write down your request on a piece of paper and tie it to the tree. Then, look up to the full moon and believe."

"Is it really that simple?"

"It is if you believe it is."

I didn't know what to believe. Maybe that was my problem: an overall lack of conviction, a general faithlessness that led me astray in times when I needed it most. I only knew what I didn't believe. My whole life was defined in negatives. But what *did* I believe?

The woman sensed my trepidation. Or maybe she noticed I wasn't writing anything down.

"Don't be afraid to heal yourself. Believe in the presence of the spirits. Become as open to giving and receiving as the spring."

I could feel the positive energy from both the spring and the tree coursing through my veins like a transfusion. It was as if the air went suddenly silent and still. All I could hear was a deep hum that I realized came from within my own body. Though my eyes were open, I couldn't see my surroundings. Instead, I could make out the faces of my ancestors. I felt their joy, their pain, their triumphs, and their tragedies. But most of all, I felt their strength. I drew a deep breath, as though it were my first. I felt cleansed and pure. In that instant, I could feel the presence of God within me, a universal force much greater than myself.

I was filled with feelings—amazing, powerful feelings—but I still had no clue what to write down. After what seemed like hours, I scribbled a few lines on the paper, tied my note among the others, and bowed my head in prayer.

As we walked away, I turned to see my message hanging from the tree. Scrawled in large letters, as if emphasizing the importance of my wish or perhaps signifying my desperation, my words filled the page:

I WISH I KNEW WHAT I BELIEVED.

Chapter 7

LADY BARBARA OF
COUNTY RIVERSIDE

"**A** man's home is his castle" may be a well-worn cliché, but to Jay, it was the gospel truth. After all, my ex-husband was in the castle-building business. As a real estate developer, he built homes for California's nouveau riche—whether they could afford those homes was another matter. But for my husband, it was more than just a way to make money; he was making dreams come true. He took a great deal of pride in that. It was one of the things I admired about him.

Nonetheless, I thought the houses he built all looked the same. They weren't castles; they were McMansions. For Jay, they were the American dream made real. For me, they were reminders of my boxed-in life. He may have been a maker of home, but I was just a homemaker.

So when I saw the brochure for a real castle at the tourist information center in Galway, I knew Ashford Castle had to be my next destination. The full-color flyer gleamed with glossy photographs of the castle—medieval stone structures, sprawling gardens, and luxurious suites. The back page pictured what looked like newlyweds on horseback. A thirteenth-century, five-star hotel with stables? I picked up my cell phone and made a reservation. Having learned my lesson about traveling in Ireland during peak season, I wasn't about to miss out on this place for the price of a phone call.

I'd planned on doing some sightseeing in Galway, but I was so excited about the castle, I went straight to Headford and drove along Lough Corrib, Ireland's second-largest lake. The Galway River connected the sea to Lough Corrib, which stretched thirty kilometers, about twenty miles, to the town of Cong in County Mayo, where Ashford Castle was located.

As I made my way north, I kept getting the feeling that I'd been there before. It wasn't a mystical feeling like I'd had at Saint Brigid's Well or a spiritual sensation—more like a fleeting feeling of recognition. Like when I couldn't remember the name of a book I'd read or match someone's face with a name. I'd seen that place before, but how and where?

My wipers intermittently swept the windshield, wiping away the mist. Every now and then, the sun teased me with a ray of hope, but a few minutes later, it ducked back into hiding.

I slowed down as the one-lane road narrowed and the trees closed in, dappling the lane with their shadows. The road turned with a curve that opened to a clearing, and there it stood—the majestic Ashford Castle, its medieval gray stonework rising from the manicured grounds. Even though I'd seen photographs, I wasn't prepared for the immense scale of the place. My little car never seemed so small! I inched across the bridge spanning the moat like a bug crawling across a leaf and halted at the looming lookout tower. A tarnished brass sign read: "Ashford Castle, 1228, County Mayo."

The castle wasn't a single edifice but a complex compound, complete with turrets and towers, nestled between forest and lawn. Beyond the grounds, the glassy waters of Lough Corrib caught a subtle reflection of the castle.

A bellman in top hat and tails greeted me as I stepped out of my car. The chain of his pocket watch dangled from his vest as he escorted me to the registration desk through a lobby decorated with antiques. I stood alone at the counter, dwarfed by the expansive foyer. Enormous chandeliers hung from the high ceiling, and oversize gilded paintings gave the castle a feeling of grandiosity. I felt terribly out of place.

The bellman waited while I checked in, then led me through red-carpeted corridors with rich mahogany walls. The corridors connected to slightly narrower passageways, a labyrinth of dark veins feeding the heart of the castle. At the peak of the tallest tower, we stopped outside my room. The massive door showed deep grooves of wear around its edges and especially around the metal handle. It looked much older than any door I'd ever seen in the States. The bellman pulled a big brass skeleton key from his pocket and unlocked the door with a clank.

"This isn't, by any chance, a haunted castle, is it?" I asked, only half joking.

The bellman chuckled. "Aye, a few ghosts roam 'round here."

I knew that some tourists who came to Ireland in search of their roots used psychics to help them connect with their pasts. While I didn't know much about the paranormal, I wondered if I could connect with my ancestors at this haunted place.

"Now, missy, I will tell ya, there are rooms here that are off-limits to guests." He lowered his voice. "Mostly because they're in the process of being restored, not because they're haunted. But around Ashford Castle, ya never know, so don't go wandering."

The bellman opened the door, and I felt a blast of cool air as I stepped across the threshold and into a chamber straight out of a fairy tale. An ornate canopy covered the four-poster bed, and tasseled curtains framed the windows with a matching fabric. Beneath the intricately carved fireplace mantle, the grate held neatly split firewood waiting for a match to bring it to life. I went to the large window that overlooked well-tended gardens and gushing fountains. Women dressed in proper English riding attire trotted along the paths, their tight pants tucked snugly into tall boots. Out on the lake, a couple rowed their boat under a crown of blooming clouds.

"It's gorgeous."

"There are mermaids and monsters to be found in Lough Corrib, so don't get any ideas to take yerself swimming."

"It looks too cold to swim." I brushed my arms to warm away the goose bumps.

"Let me light the fire for you, missy. We're expecting rain."

I smiled. Since I lived in the Southern California desert, I welcomed both the green landscape and the rain that came with it.

After the bellman left, I fought off the temptation to twirl around the room. Next to the bed, piled luxuriantly high with a down comforter and satin pillows, a ceramic bowl filled with fresh fruit stood on the nightstand. On the dresser, a crystal decanter of sherry glinted in the firelight.

I changed into my best travel clothes, but they didn't seem elegant enough for my resplendent surroundings. Feeling like Scarlett O'Hara, I descended the spiral staircase to the restaurant. The candlelit tables were set with sparkling crystal and bone china. I glanced at the menu on display at the hostess station. A prix fixe five-course meal featuring pheasant, duck, or lamb. I wondered what my great-great-grandmother would think if she could see me now. She'd probably rejoice in knowing that her voyage to America in search of a better life had paid off for her descendants. Five generations of hard work and good luck had left Lady Barbara of County Riverside a long, long way from the Great Famine. If Grandma Pat were at Ashford Castle, she'd skip the fine dining and opt for a bit of local flavor. So that's what I did.

A soft rain began to fall, blurring the edges of the lake and the forest. I borrowed an umbrella from the front desk and set off down the road to Cong. The feeling I'd had on the road of having been there before returned. I inhaled the fragrant scent of the damp woods. Though the crisp air chilled my cheeks and made my nose run a bit, it didn't matter. Like the bellman said, people didn't come to Ireland for the weather. I felt immersed in history. If a horseman dressed in clothes one hundred, two hundred, five hundred years out of date came clomping past on his steed, I don't think it would have fazed me a bit.

As I strolled into town, villagers greeted me: young women pushing prams, teenagers sporting rugby shirts, older gents in their thick sweaters and tweed caps. I stepped into a pub. Behind the bar hung a large, framed poster of my ex-husband's hero and namesake, John Wayne, in *The Quiet Man*. Jay's friends called him "The Duke" when we were first married, a real man's man.

That was it! That was why the place seemed so familiar. I ordered a pint—the universal connector—and learned that in the 1950s, the director John Ford had fallen in love with Cong and Ashford Castle and had shot much of *The Quiet Man* there. I had to laugh. I'd come to Ireland to find a new Barbara, but vestiges of my old life lurked around every corner.

One by one, amateur musicians drew out their instruments: fiddle, accordion, tin whistle, *bodhrán*—a large goat-skinned drum. Together, the group drifted into an impromptu jam session called a *céile*, playing an assortment of jigs, reels, hornpipes, and ballads that everyone knew by heart. I thought of the diners back at the castle, clinking their silverware on china plates. I thought about Naidra, the six-fingered Wiccan, granting wishes at a sacred well. I thought of my ex-husband, sitting in front of a flat-screen television watching dusty westerns and sipping Scotch. I thought of Grandma Pat, naked as a jaybird, her head thrown back in laughter, having the time of her life, and I knew, for once I'd made the right decision. Ireland finally felt like home.

—⁓—

The next morning, I threw off my comforter, tossed aside my pillows, and jumped into my riding gear. Ashford Castle featured a world-renowned equestrian center, and I planned to make the most of its excellent riding facilities. I wanted to explore as much of the grounds on horseback as I could.

Even though the sun finally made an appearance and a colorful rainbow arced across the sky, the stables were deserted except for a man brushing the thick mane of a Connemara pony. He looked up and flashed an easy smile as I approached. His eyes danced with the kind of mischief that made me want to misbehave.

"Yes, ma'am, can I help ya?" he asked, politely tipping his hat.

"I'd like to rent a horse for the day."

"I take it ya know how to ride." I could feel him giving me the once-over.

"Oh, yes," I answered. "I've been doing it since I was a kid." I became aware of the double meaning behind "ride" and "doing it" and blushed like a schoolgirl, but he appeared not to notice.

"Grand. What kind of beast suits ya?"

"What have you got?"

"Let me show you. I'm Patrick, by the way," he said, extending his hand as he led me toward the stalls. "Named after the favorite saint of my mother, may God rest her soul."

Patrick must have been around forty, with a shock of red hair and endearing freckles sprinkled across his nose. As I followed him to the back of the stable, sun shone into the stalls in stripes of light broken up by the iron grates in the windows.

"Aye. Here we go. This is Rusty. He's a gentle Irish Sport Horse that jumps well and knows these trails like the back of his—"

"Hoof?"

Patrick laughed as I took the reins. Rusty was a big chestnut gelding, larger than the Connemara I rode with Fiona, but I barely noticed him, I was so smitten by Patrick's charming laugh and crooked smile.

"So, are you my guide for the day?" I asked, taking a chance.

"Well, now, I could see my way clear to do that. I think Francis can handle things here without me." He gestured over his shoulder to a man hauling saddles from behind the barn. "Hey, Francis! I'm going to take the beautiful young lady out for a ride. Think ya can manage?"

"Aye!" he called back.

While Patrick saddled our horses in traditional English tack, I felt a hum running through my body. My thoughts drifted back to those lazy days in Riverside with Carson. I didn't want to come all the way to Ireland just to make the same mistake, but I felt deliciously free, and the castle grounds put me smack in the middle of a storybook setting. Perhaps I had even found myself a prince. What did I have to lose?

I mounted my horse and followed Patrick down a road almost hidden by the dense woodlands. The steady rhythm of Rusty's gait transported me to the pages of a fairy tale. I imagined strange creatures around every corner. The road narrowed to a trail, and in some areas, the forest was so thick that Patrick had to use a riding crop to beat back the trees and forge a path. He explained that Sir Benjamin Lee Guinness had taken great pride in the forest, planting thousands of trees on the grounds. I made a mental note to toast Sir Guinness during my next visit to the pub.

When we rode through the forest and emerged back onto the road, a group of cyclists passed us, huffing mightily as they pedaled with their heads bowed low. I was grateful to have a higher view of the rolling green hills and cottages—and a horse that did all the work. Once we passed the neighboring villages, we ran the horses into the open countryside. Patrick jumped his horse over an old stone fence, and I followed without hesitation, eager to show him that I was his equal astride a horse. I leaned forward and neatly cleared the rocky obstacle. I wanted to prove that I was more than just a pretty face. I wanted Patrick to know that I was competent in the saddle. If he played his cards right, I might even take *him* for a ride.

The feeling of timelessness that had filled me in Dingle returned. There seemed to be no escaping it. I'd come to Ireland to figure out what to do next with my life, to chart a path for my future, yet I kept moving backward in time, not forward. Why fight it? Maybe I'd lived there in a past life, and I'd been summoned to experience things as they'd been hundreds or even thousands of years earlier.

During the ride, Patrick and I chatted amiably, swapping flirtatious looks whenever our horses walked abreast. I could feel him undressing me with his eyes, and in a fair exchange, I slowly stripped him down in my imagination.

In addition to working at the stables, Patrick hunted foxes, something he'd done since he was a boy. He seemed to take great pleasure in describing hunting techniques to me, from the methods for training the dogs to strategies for capturing the elusive animals known for their lustrous red coats. Irish Sport Horses, like the one I rode that day, were skilled jumpers, so the breed was often used in fox hunting. He said the hunt was like a contest—a match of wits, strength, speed, and agility. I laughed to myself. Did he know that he was on another hunting trip, only this time he was the quarry?

"Sounds like an excuse to be outdoors all day," I said.

"Sometimes the greatest pleasures are found in the simplest things."

I was learning this the hard way, and I hoped that my toughest lessons were behind me. After several hours, we headed back to the stable. I felt tired, but it was a good tired, and I looked forward to a hot soak in the claw-foot tub back in what I thought of as "my chambers."

"Thanks for such a lovely day, Patrick."

"My pleasure. Hope you come back." He grasped my extended hand, then bent his head to kiss it. Charming!

I laughed and rubbed Rusty, who snorted in appreciation. Leaving the stable, I wondered if Patrick was married. I hadn't seen a ring, though that didn't necessarily mean anything. I wanted to be wanted, to spend time with someone who was interested in *me*. Another day of riding might speed things along.

As I crossed the grounds on my way back to the castle, I passed a sign that read: "Ireland's School of Falconry." I looked through the gate and saw rows of wire cages filled with large birds. I could hear them ruffling their feathers and making soft sounds, muffled *coo*s and *caw*s. Curious, I pushed through the gate and walked in.

"Hello there!" a voice called out.

Startled, I spun around. A tall man stood a few feet from me. Though his expression was friendly, I felt like a trespasser. He rested a gloved hand on top of one of the cages, and the huge bird inside fluttered its wings in what looked more like annoyance than fear.

"I'm sorry," I said. "I'm staying at the castle." I felt a bit like I was in a zoo or a wildlife refuge, surrounded by all those birds. The air held a sharp, pungent odor, but the humidity made it smell almost sweet.

"Are you enjoying your stay?" he asked as he pulled off the gauntlet glove and offered his hand. "I'm Daniel."

"I got here only yesterday, but so far, it's been fabulous. I hope you don't mind me poking around."

Daniel shook his head. "Not at all." His thick black hair almost hid his dark eyes. He appeared younger than Patrick but was every bit as handsome. Maybe even more so. Another prince.

I squeezed between two cages to get a closer look at the birds. A stout wire grid formed enclosures that were several feet tall. They were clean and roomy, with several perches inside.

Daniel walked over to a small table where food for the raptors was spread out on dented metal trays. I flinched and swallowed hard to keep my lunch from coming up when I saw the stiff shapes of field mice, rats, and even rabbits. Daniel nonchalantly picked up a few dead rodents and placed the carcasses inside the birdcages, selecting larger rodents for the bigger birds. His large hands looked nimble as he doled out the food.

"So is this what you do here?" I asked. "Feed dead animals to the birds?" I jumped when a caged owl behind me let out an unsolicited screech.

"Aye," he said. "I train predatory birds like falcons, eagles, and owls. Here at the School of Falconry, we try to provide the birds with their natural diet, even in captivity."

"Train them for what?"

"Falconers train birds to return with their prey. The practice of falconry is an ancient art. Some say it's the oldest sport in the world. We train them to scare sea gulls and crows away from agricultural fields, instead of using pesticides. They work hand in hand with Mother Nature." His dark eyes were direct but not flirtatious as he fed me another tidbit.

"Did you know that most falcons mate for life? The females play the dominant role."

"That's ..." I struggled for the right word, "interesting." My thoughts went back to the Celtic church service and the Wiccans. The Irish had a way of validating the worth of the feminine, nurturing Mother Nature so she could nurture them in return. I felt the power of being a woman. This stranger's hint at the attractiveness of dominant females gave me confidence in myself.

"Would you like to see how the art of falconry works?" he asked.

"I'd love to."

Daniel reached into a cage and placed his gloved hand beneath a bird hunched atop its perch. As the raptor swiveled its smooth head, I caught the flash of its sharply hooked beak and talons. It gave me the willies when I thought of how easily the bird could rip apart its prey, but Daniel didn't seem to give this a second thought.

"Falconry originated as a hunting sport," he explained. "The birds were trained to hunt small game, and when a falcon returned with its prey, the hunter would persuade the bird to release its catch by offering it a small piece of raw meat. We use this same technique to reward the birds when they properly return to an outstretched arm."

He raised his hand a little closer to the perch until the falcon alighted with an impressive beating of its wings. Daniel withdrew his hand from the cage, and as the bird fought for balance, its primaries spread like hairy fingers, subtly striated in countless shades of brown. Daniel quickly extended his arm to keep from being batted in the face by the bird's powerful wings.

"Let's take a walk," Daniel said, grabbing a spare leather glove.

I thought maybe he was talking to the bird, not me, but I followed him outside anyway. The falcon hopped its way up Daniel's forearm, which was sheathed in protective leather. Outside, Daniel lifted his arm, and the falcon took flight, propelled into heaven with an effortless flap of its wings. I was glad the sky was blue, but even against the clear sky, I had a hard time tracking the bird as it soared high above. After a few minutes, Daniel placed his arm out like a branch, holding a small piece of raw meat in his gloved hand. Silently bidden, the falcon returned to perch on Daniel's outstretched arm.

"Amazing," I said. "How long have you been doing this?"

"I think birds swirled around my crib. Would you like to give it a try?"

"Me?" I stammered. "I wouldn't know what to do."

"Just put this on your arm," he said. The stiff glove he handed me was heavy, with rough seams that chafed against my skin, but I was thrilled to be wearing it when Daniel put his arm next to mine and gave the bird a gentle nudge. The leather gauntlet extended to my elbow, protecting me from the bird's razor-sharp talons.

The magnificent creature that was perched on my forearm weighed much more than I expected. My arm was nowhere near as long as Daniel's, so the bird sat fairly close to my face. I marveled at the impossibly intricate pattern that covered the falcon in feathers. Only its legs and feet were feather-free. On the falcon's left leg, a leather strap attached some sort of transmitter.

"What's that for?" I asked.

"That's so we can monitor its altitude," Daniel said.

Intimidated by the bird and its curved beak, I launched the falcon into flight with a nervous shake of my hand. I watched jealously as it climbed high above the earth.

After a few minutes, Daniel placed a piece of raw meat in my gloved hand. "You bond with the bird by feeding it," he said.

I held the meat gingerly and stretched out my arm like a branch. A very nervous branch. The raptor returned at the signal and landed on my arm, gobbling up its reward and defiantly staring at me with its glassy eyes. I stared back as the chunk of meat disappeared down the bird's gullet. When the feeding falcon recognized me as a partner, not a predator, it seemed to relax, sinking down into a resting pose on my arm. I felt its talons through the leather and imagined my forearm dotted with little puncture wounds. When I launched the falcon again, I quickly removed the glove for a look at my arm. Not a mark on it!

After working with the falcon for nearly an hour, Daniel and I walked back toward the school, where I reluctantly returned the raptor to its cage. I heard the muffled rustle of plumage as Daniel took out an eagle, which had fine feathers that swept back from its head to its tail in perfect alignment.

"Eagles can weigh up to seven kilos," Daniel said. "They're much larger than falcons."

I was no expert in metric conversions, but I guessed that seven kilos was somewhere around fifteen pounds. The huge eagle was bold and stately, but I favored the falcon, perhaps because it was my first experience with a raptor.

Back outside, we repeated the flying and feeding routine with the eagle. Next, we exercised an owl. Though it wasn't quite as majestic as the falcon or the eagle, the owl moved with a furtive grace that I found enchanting. It flew in utter silence, even when taking off and landing. Its huge eyes were so perfectly round that they seemed almost fake, but I was convinced of their reality when they blinked just inches from my face.

"The owl has a special place in Celtic tradition," Daniel explained. "It represents many things, including wisdom, stealth, initiation, and change."

Perhaps my visit to the School of Falconry was a portent of change to come. Patrick faded from my memory as I watched Daniel put the birds back in their cages.

"Two hours just flew by!"

"No pun intended," Daniel said as he shut the last cage door. He stripped off his glove, and I noticed the well-defined muscles of his forearm. "Stop by anytime."

"I will," I said and meant it.

Two invitations, two men wanting to please me: fair-skinned Patrick and dark-eyed Daniel.

—⁂—

Back in my room, I filled the oversize tub with bath salts and scented bubbles. I stepped in with a glass of wine and sat back to reflect on my day. Horses, raptors, rodents, and men. The rodents I could do without, but the rest fueled my passions and intrigued me. What was it about Ireland? There was magic in the air.

I wanted to share my experiences with someone, but I couldn't think of anyone who would relate. My friends and family back in the States were too far removed, both physically and emotionally. I wanted a companion, and I wanted one *right now*.

To make matters worse, there was a wedding taking place down in the gardens below. I always dreamed of a fairy-tale wedding, and that one looked like something straight out of a storybook. The petite bride took short steps across the grass, trailing her ruffled train. Her dark hair, piled high atop her head, shone with subtle shades of red. The groom stood tall and confident, waiting for her under a vine-covered arbor. I imagined Patrick with a carriage and a team of horses ready to sweep the happy couple away. Or Daniel, standing at the ready to release a pair of falcons carrying bundles of rose petals to drop upon the happy couple the moment they were pronounced husband and wife.

Inevitably, the scene brought back memories of my own marriage.

As a little girl, I imagined the man I'd marry. He'd be handsome, charming, and of course, he'd treat me like a princess. As I got older, my dream changed to reflect my grandparents' relationship—a festive union marked by deep respect. Later, my vision morphed again into one that matched my parents' tie—a steady but somewhat dull partnership enriched by shared experiences.

From the first time I met him at a college mixer, I knew Jay was the man who could fulfill the role I had already scripted for my husband. If it had been a play, it would have been called "How to Follow in Your Mother's Footsteps." Of course, my parents adored Jay, a handsome fellow from a good family, and a hardworking businessman, successful even in his youth.

In 1978, I was a sophomore at Fresno State. I lived at Kappa Alpha Theta with my sixty sorority sisters. One of them was dating an older guy who lived off campus. That spring, he had a little get-together. Scratch that—he threw a party. Because he was my sorority sister's boyfriend, I went—and felt entirely out of place. I had no date and knew no one except my girlfriend, who disappeared in search of her beau as soon as we walked in. Ever the obedient Barbara, I did everything I was supposed to do and nothing that I wasn't. I sat in a corner sipping a Coke and feeling out of my element among that sophisticated crowd, with their unfiltered cigarettes and martinis shaken, not stirred.

Then, Jay stepped in.

He picked up an icy cocktail from the makeshift bar, then leaned against the wall, staring at me, a cocky grin on his face. Just when I thought I wouldn't be able to take another second of it, he strutted across the room, bent down so his face was merely inches from mine, and introduced himself.

He was six-foot-two, with piercing blue eyes. A thick mustache drooped around the corners of his mouth and barely touched the edge of his upper lip. He was suave enough to charm my socks off—and maybe some other things, too. We spent the rest of the evening talking, and I giggled nervously when he asked for my number so he could "call me sometime." Later that night, safely tucked into my bed at the sorority house, surrounded by restless virgins, I fell asleep thinking about him.

"Sometime" turned out to be the next day. He invited me to dinner and a movie the following weekend.

The night of our date, I changed my outfit four times, unhappy with every dress in my closet. Finally, I settled on a black shift, low heels, and a delicate gold necklace. I fluffed up my hair and emptied half a can of Aquanet into it.

"There's a tall drink of water waiting for you downstairs," my roommate Marie announced with a sly grin. "Better go get him before a sister gulps him down."

"Tell him I'll be right there!"

I took several deep breaths as I tiptoed down the steps to the sorority lobby, trying to calm the roaring in my ears. Jay was standing next to the front door in a Western blazer, crisp white shirt, and a pair of neatly pressed Wranglers. As we walked out to the car, I knew the other girls were watching enviously. Like a gentleman, Jay opened the door of his convertible to let me in. I slid onto the smooth leather seat and arranged my dress, then touched my hair to ensure it was securely sprayed in place. It was a perfect convertible night. *Thank you, Aquanet!*

On the way to The Refectory, a popular Fresno restaurant, Jay and I spoke of our families and asked each other about our plans for the summer. He rested his hand on my thigh as he drove, and my heart rate rose a few notches. At the restaurant, a valet took the car. I'd never been to a place where you paid someone to park your car. Jay held my hand and guided me inside.

The hostess sat us at a quiet table next to the window. I looked around. It was fancy—white tablecloths and candles graced every table, and most of the patrons were enjoying wine with their meals. As I sat across from Jay, I felt suddenly shy. It was one thing to be careening down the street in a car with the wind in my face, but it was something else entirely to be sitting still, afraid of saying the wrong thing or, even worse, not knowing what to say at all.

"Dollar for your thoughts," he said.

"Isn't it a penny?"

He laughed. "I don't believe in pennies. I always think big."

Jay in a nutshell.

A soft murmur of voices drifted over from the nearby tables in an energetic buzz. People came to The Refectory for more than just the food. The place had a cozy, welcoming atmosphere that encouraged guests to linger over their meals.

Jay asked me what I was studying, and I told him about physical therapy and how I'd spent the summer working in a home for disabled children in the Canary Islands. When I was in high school, I traveled with my church to Mexico, where I interned as a physical therapist. I desperately wanted to show him that I'd seen more of the world than just Fresno.

He didn't say anything. He just stared at me. Feeling self-conscious, my hand flew to the bird's nest that was my hair. "Is something wrong?" I asked.

"I'm sorry," he said. "I just can't stop looking at you. You're so beautiful."

I felt myself blush at his words, and my heart ricocheted around inside my chest. Fumbling for my water glass, I took a sip. And then another. I didn't even say thank you. I just stared at my menu, but I needn't have bothered. When the waiter appeared in his starched white apron, Jay ordered for both of us, including wine. I was relieved. I didn't recognize most of the things on the menu, and I was grateful for the way he automatically took charge.

Alcohol was forbidden in the house where I grew up, and I'd never had so much as a taste of wine, let alone a whole glass. I was anxious and afraid. What if they asked for my ID? What if I were caught? What would my parents say? When the waiter returned with two glasses of wine, Jay picked up his by the stem and raised it in the air. I followed suit.

"Here's to a great first date," he said as we clinked our glasses together. "And many more."

I took a sip of the red elixir, not knowing what to expect. My first impression was that the wine tasted a bit like vinegar, but it went down smooth and slowly warmed the inside of my mouth, leaving a little tingle on my tongue.

Was it all that easy? Around Jay, it certainly seemed to be the way things worked. I knew right then that I wanted to be his wife.

Jay was four years my senior, though to me we seemed decades apart. Even at a young age, he had an authoritative air about him. Among his inner circle, he was the de facto leader, and everyone, myself included, looked up to him for advice, for approval, for everything. Just a few months from graduating, he seemed well on his way to becoming a success. He was worldly and sophisticated, even then. He took me to parties and concerts and brought me into his wide circle of friends. He was at ease in almost any social situation. There seemed to be nothing he didn't know. He could make a joke out of anything—or anyone. Being with Jay was like taking your first trip to New York City: the sights, sounds, and smells overwhelmed you, and you knew you'd never encounter anything like it again.

Ours was a relationship of firsts. He wasn't the first boy I ever kissed, but he was my first serious boyfriend, and the first man I slept with. He took great pride and satisfaction in the fact that I was a virgin. When I was with him, forbidden things didn't seem so evil. It was easy to break the rules.

Jay's penchant for the cowboy way also attracted me to him. Not only did he look and dress like a wrangler, but his family also owned a horse ranch in Merced that spilled into the foothills of the Sierra Nevada. While I was fortunate enough to be able to ride regularly in my youth, the neighborhood stable was a public facility. I couldn't imagine living on a ranch and being surrounded by horses.

On Christmas Eve of my senior year, Jay proposed. We spent the holiday with his folks on their ranch. After a family dinner of baked ham with all the fixings, we adjourned to the living room and sat around the tree. Jay dropped to one knee and produced a black velvet box. I opened it slowly, unsure if it was a Christmas gift or "the ring."

The box held an engagement ring, set with his grandmother's diamond. He'd chosen the setting himself, independent to the core.

"Will you marry me?" he asked.

I screamed out an enthusiastic "Yes!" to the claps and delight of his family. I was too blind to see that I was on the verge of stepping into his world, becoming completely his and his alone.

We were wed in my childhood church. I wore a traditional, high-necked Victorian gown and long, fingerless gloves. My mother cried as my father walked me down the aisle. I had eight bridesmaids, and over one hundred and fifty guests packed the pews. It was all very proper and predictable, just like he wanted.

Before the wedding, Grandma Pat had asked me why I wanted to marry so young and sign up for the role of wife before I had even auditioned as an independent woman.

I didn't have an answer for her.

My mom said, "He'll take care of you." I think this put her at ease, knowing that I would be well provided for once I left her home to start a family of my own.

The strangest thing about my wedding day is that I have absolutely no recollection of how I felt. I remember details like the chocolate cake and the pink flowers, but I have no memory of feeling joyful, nervous, weepy, or any of the things brides are supposed to feel on their special day. I know I must have felt *something* that day, but what? Had I blocked these memories out when my marriage started to sour? Or was it because, when I got married, I was simply doing what I was "supposed" to be doing, going through the motions?

Watching the couple exchange vows in the garden at Ashford Castle, a strange kind of melancholy overcame me. I was keenly aware of the things I *didn't* feel on my wedding day—excited, liberated, and free. I raised my glass to the happy couple. The young bride and groom had their whole lives ahead of them; the totality of their future was an open road rising up to meet them—just like in the Irish blessing.

But what about me? Where would the road take me? Was I destined to travel it alone? Would I meet an equal partner who accepted me for who I was? Was there a prince out there for me?

Chapter 8

HOW HIGH THE MOON

I wandered back and forth between my palatial suite and the balcony overlooking the lake and the wedding below. My chambers were so enormous that I had a hard time deciding where to sit. After a few minutes in a wing-backed chair next to the fireplace, I returned to the balcony. I brushed away the vague memories I had of my own wedding and reminded myself that I was single, free to be with another man. Although I was a little nervous, I was eager to initiate a new relationship, even if it was only a fling. I debated which man I should invite to dinner, vacillating between Patrick the fair-featured equestrian and Daniel the dark-haired falconer.

Many times I have wished for an indication, no matter how big or small, that the step I was about to take was the right one. Just a cosmic nudge to let me know I was on the right path. But no matter how intently I searched, the sign I hoped for rarely revealed itself to me. I was thinking about the old saying, "Be careful what you wish for," when a large owl alighted on my balcony railing, scaring the bejesus out of me.

I'd like to say I let out a delicate squeal of delight, but in truth, I screamed my bloody head off and retreated inside the room, slamming the door behind me. The owl stayed around, locking its eyes with mine through the glass door. I had always thought owls were cute when I saw them in photographs, but when this one dropped onto my balcony, I felt as if a winged monkey from *The Wizard of Oz* had come to carry me off.

In reality, this owl had probably gotten loose from the School of Falconry. It might have even been the one I had worked with earlier that afternoon. Still, it seemed to have a message for me. I'd been thinking about which Irishman to ring. Did the owl's arrival mean I should choose its handler, Daniel? After all, hadn't Daniel told me that owls represent change? What was that wise bird trying to tell me?

The owl sat perched on the balcony, swiveling its head from side to side. At one point, it seemed to catch its own reflection in the glass door and cocked its head inquisitively. Then it occurred to me that Daniel might have sent the owl to my room on purpose. A clever way of making sure I was thinking of him. Could he send birds to do his bidding like that? Would he?

The owl stirred and, in a silent beating of wings whose motion startled me all over again, ascended into the air. It glided out over the lake and disappeared in the gathering dusk. Just like that, it was gone. I began to doubt it was ever there.

I wondered again if Daniel had manifested the owl's presence. If he had, it didn't bother me. Just the opposite. While Patrick was attractive, and I'd felt a bit of chemistry with him during our ride that morning, he was too much of a charmer. Daniel, on the other hand, was more circumspect. He was more my type physically, and although we'd had a nice afternoon together, he didn't press for my attention.

I got the number for the School of Falconry from the front desk and paced the room, working up the nerve to ring Daniel. I don't know why I felt such trepidation. I was an attractive single woman traveling alone. I was staying in a gorgeous room, and I wanted to share it with someone. It made all the sense in the world. Why wouldn't I crave some company in a situation like that? I was lonely. And I had energy to release. Put the two together and you get desperate. That wasn't what I wanted to be. I didn't come all the way to Ireland to play out romance novel fantasies. Lady Barbara and the Falconer.

Yet, I could hear Grandma Pat's voice. *Oh, for heaven's sake, Barbara, it's just a phone call.* At that moment, I brushed the image of my naked grandmother aside, picked up the phone, and dialed.

"Hello," answered a man in a thick accent.

"Daniel?" I asked. I hadn't remembered his accent sounding like that.

"Sorry. He's gone for the day." The way this man said "sorry" made me wonder if he was a Brit.

"Oh," I said and sank down onto the bed, utterly deflated. So much for my brave advances into a new relationship.

"Help you with something?" the man asked.

Something in my tone of voice must have betrayed my disappointment, because he sounded genuine and sincere. I paced around the expansive suite with the cordless phone to my ear. "I was going to ask Daniel out for dinner, but I guess I'm too late."

"Are you the bird I saw working with Daniel at the school today?"

"Yes," I answered. "My name's Barb."

"Well, Barb, you did miss Daniel, but why don't you have dinner with me?"

"Excuse me?" I wasn't sure if I'd heard him correctly. I hadn't seen anyone else at the school when I'd been there, but apparently, someone had seen *me*. And he had just asked me out for dinner. A complete stranger. I sat down on the overstuffed loveseat.

"What's your name?"

"My name's Derek, and I give great customer service."

I laughed at the joke. Had Daniel told him about our afternoon together? If so, that wouldn't make him a *complete* stranger.

"Okay," I squeaked.

"Right, then," he said. "I'll meet you in an hour at the Crowe's

Nest. It's a pub down the road just a spot, walking distance. You'll be safe. No worries."

A pub? I guess it made sense. Hotel employees were probably discouraged from fraternizing with the guests, especially on hotel property. I hung up the phone, wondering what the hell I'd just agreed to. I'd been accused of being impulsive before, but a blind date with a foreigner in a pub brought things to a whole new level. What if Derek was a doddering old troll? What if he was a bona fide creep?

I needed a fallback plan, a way out, in case things got weird down at the pub. I phoned the front desk and arranged for the hotel's car service to pick me up at the Crowe's Nest half an hour after I was scheduled to arrive. That way, if I walked into the pub and got a bad vibe, I could march right back out to a safe car whose driver would whisk me back to my fairy tale.

My little black dress was too "little" for the evening chill, and it didn't offer any protection from the eternally soft weather and dripping trees. On my way out, I stopped by the castle gift shop to see if they had some kind of wrap and purchased a black wool cape. Perfect! In my mind, I looked just like Maureen O'Hara, John Wayne's costar in *The Quiet Man*.

I took off for town, walking by the old buildings that lined the winding cobblestone streets. A butcher, a tailor, a candy shop, a news vendor. All of them were closed for the day. Tall, narrow houses of stone and whitewashed timber stood like picturesque pages from a guidebook.

In ten minutes, I arrived at the Crowe's Nest and quickly scanned the room. The only other patrons were a young couple tucked into a corner and an old man, pipe in hand, who paid me no mind. Heavy wooden beams supported the low ceiling of the dark pub, and the aroma of fried food drifted from the kitchen. It appeared that Derek had not yet arrived. I chose a table near the back and ordered a Guinness. Whenever the door to the pub opened, my head snapped up in anticipation. Each time, the entrance proffered a rollicking couple or a bleary-eyed man stopping in for a pint of Ireland's black gold.

Just when I thought I'd been stood up, a single man who looked to be in his early thirties entered the pub. He strolled up to the bar and leaned against it while he surveyed the scene. My breath caught in my throat. He wore a tweed jacket and a wool cap; a plaid scarf hung around his neck, and blond hair framed his face in wavy curls. He exuded raw, male energy. His eyes caught mine, and his face relaxed into an easy grin as he walked toward my table.

"Waiting for a date?" he asked, his green eyes catching the light. They twinkled like a sign that said, "Open for business."

"Not a date. A dinner companion named Derek."

"Well, you found him," he said. "Daniel is a bloody good bloke. I've known him for years, but I'm glad he couldn't make it."

I'd only know Daniel for an afternoon, but I, too, was suddenly grateful that he had already been gone by the time I called. I squinted at Derek as he spoke. His accent wasn't an Irish brogue.

"You're not Irish, are you?"

"Nope. A Brit. Born and raised in London."

Whatever. Irish or British, handsome and charming were handsome and charming, and I wasn't about to turn him away. Derek went to the bar to get a Guinness of his own, and when the waitress showed up a few minutes later, we ordered standard pub fare—toasties with cheese, tomatoes, and onions. I had grown fond of the classic Irish comfort food, which was basically grilled cheese sandwiches with a few extra ingredients thrown in for good measure. Of course, they were served with the ubiquitous fried potato wedges they call chips.

I talked about life in California, and Derek told me about growing up in London and working with falcons for the Harry Potter movies. He had studied the symbolism of owls as well as how they lived in nature.

"The owl can see what others can't," he explained. "Wiccans interpret this with a slightly deeper meaning. They believe that the owl can see through deception, seeking truth and wisdom."

"I had a visit from an owl tonight," I said, wondering if Derek would find this unusual.

"You were lucky. Some say that owls will only visit those who share the same energy with them."

I felt a little tug inside. Derek had an inquisitive and open mind to go along with his good looks. I glanced at my watch. The hotel's service car was probably waiting for me out front. I excused myself and dashed out to tell the driver thanks, but no thanks. When I returned to the table, we picked up where we left off. I found his British accent romantic. It was easier for me to understand than the Irish brogue, and I asked questions just to hear him talk. I started to feel a little light-headed. Was it the strong Irish brew or the strong British man? I didn't care which. It felt delicious.

After dinner, we lingered over Irish coffee. He laughed when I told of my tales of how I came to Ireland, lost my luggage, drove a toy car, and met a witch.

"The leprechauns here have played some tricks on you," he said.

"I'm learning to live more spontaneously and just go with the flow."

He smiled and leaned close. "You know, John Wayne drank at this—"

"I didn't come to hear stories about John Wayne," I said, putting my finger to his lips. At first I thought I'd been too bold, that I offended him somehow, but Derek smiled that easy smile of his.

"Come with me," he whispered. "I want to show you the moon."

As Derek led me out of the pub, my conscience flipped between feelings of lust and caution—lust the voice of Grandma Pat, caution the voice of my mother. But lust easily got the better of caution. I tightened my grip on Derek's calloused hand, aroused by the masculine feel of it. He probably labored outdoors every day, putting in honest work that made him sweat. I loved the sensation of his rough palm against my soft skin, and I drew myself a little closer to his side as we walked down the street in the brisk night air. Derek's car was parked on the corner, and floating on the heady Guinness and Derek's potent charms, I cast caution to the wind and climbed in.

"Where are we going?" I asked.

He grinned. "It's a surprise."

I tried not to think about all the horrible things that could happen to a woman alone in a foreign country, leaving a pub with a stranger, clueless about where he was taking her. The chatter in my mind died down, and after a deep breath, I realized I wasn't afraid at all. My nerves were definitely tingling, but I attributed that to the man at the wheel.

Derek pulled off the main street onto a tiny, unpaved road. After a short, bumpy ride we came to a stop in what looked like the middle of nowhere. Derek turned off the engine and ran around to the left side of the car to open my door. He held out his hand like a gentleman.

"Are you ready?" he asked.

I placed my hand in his and stepped out of the car. He held a "torch" in his other hand and used the flashlight to guide us through tall grass and low shrubs, down to what I realized was Lough Corrib. We walked for a bit before we came to a clearing where I could see the light of the moon, the same moon that had lit up the night at Saint Brigid's Well. Like a giant floodlight, it illuminated the lake, glimmering on the surface of the still black water. I stopped, overwhelmed by its beauty.

Derek tugged on my hand. "Come on," he said as he led me onto a boat dock. He tucked the flashlight, now completely unnecessary, into his pocket. He wrapped his arms around me and held me close. I could hear the lapping of gentle waves against the dock's pilings.

"This is the moon I wanted you to see," Derek said.

"I've seen the moon a million times, but never like this." It felt as if I were caught in a cliché. I couldn't stop saying terribly cheesy things, and I thought I might chase Derek away by proving what a brainless Yank I was. But I couldn't help it.

When Derek turned me around and pressed his chest against my back, I gasped. His strong arms locked me tightly in his grasp. The scent of his aftershave and the fine stubble of his cheek sent shivers up my spine. I couldn't see his face, couldn't move my arms. For a moment, I thought about midnight stranglers and wondered what the Irish version of Scotland Yard was called. He's not … He wouldn't … But when he turned me around, I realized that he was leading me in a dance, accompanied by the soothing symphony of bullfrogs and crickets. I breathed deeply, taking in the organic smell of the lake water. But if Derek thought I was going to lie down in the grass so he could rip my bodice open, he had another think coming.

"Come on," he said after a few rounds on the floating dance floor. "Let's go back to Ashford Castle."

"Okay," I whispered.

He drove back up the gravel road and through town to the castle. We walked into the lobby hand in hand, still feeling the magic of the night. Soft light glowed from dimmed chandeliers and ornate sconces. Passing by the front desk, we started down the maze of corridors.

"Let's explore a little bit," he said. "Open the doors they say to keep closed …"

"You mean chase ghosts?"

"Maybe," he said with a wink that devastated me. I'd never been undone by a man's eyelashes before.

Against the bellman's warning, we rambled around the castle's many floors. Derek took the flashlight out of his pocket, and we crept through tunnels and passageways. When we came upon unnumbered doors, we tried the handles. One door led to a massive mechanical room that smelled of heating oil and cleaning solutions. Another led to an old storage room, filled with dusty antiques and musty linens. An old tablecloth hung near the back of the room, looking eerily like a ghost.

At the end of the second-floor hallway, we found a dark staircase and ascended until we could go no higher. To the right of the staircase, a small crevice opened into the night, and cool, damp air breathed into the castle.

"Come on," Derek said, squeezing sideways through the narrow passage.

He held out his hand and guided me through the cleft in the stone wall. We emerged onto a balcony, high above the lake, safe in a forbidden place. I felt like a rescued Rapunzel.

The sky twinkled, and I watched in vain for a falling star to wish upon, then wished anyway.

"Have you ever had a wish come true?" I asked Derek.

"Lots of 'em," he said. "I think about what I want, make a wish, and before I know it, my wish has come true. There's some universal power that just makes it work."

I wanted that power. I wanted that man. I tugged at Derek's sleeve when the chill began to make me shiver. We went back inside, retracing our route without seeing any spirits or specters. But Derek did perform a magic trick of sorts, for at the end of our tour, we stood outside my door.

"I had a lovely time tonight," he said. He grinned at me, and the corners of his eyes smiled, too. Could he have been any more captivating?

"So did I. Thank you for dinner. And thank you for the moon."

He leaned down and kissed me, softly at first, then deeply, his tongue probing my mouth. My heart fluttered, and I sensed that forgotten hum between my legs. His kiss was just like the rest of him: assertive but gentle, and very sexy. He pulled back and winked.

"Well ... good night," he said and moved to go.

I placed a hand on his arm. "You don't have to leave."

"Are you sure?"

I nodded, slipping the big black key out of my purse and turning it in the lock. We stepped inside and came together for another kiss. I fumbled with the doorknob in search of the "Do Not Disturb" sign, found it, and just managed to twist it around the handle before Derek kicked the door closed. My cape fell to the floor, leaving me standing in my little black dress. His hands roamed lightly over the peaks of my breasts, his lips warm and fleshy against my own. I let out a soft moan and pressed myself closer to him. I slid my hand between his legs and let my fingers graze against him with gentle pressure. It was his turn to moan as he held my face in his hands.

"Has anyone ever told you how sexy you are?" he whispered between kisses.

I didn't answer. In my twenty-three years of marriage to Jay, sex appeal wasn't part of the equation. Sensuality wasn't something he valued, so that part of me had languished.

"You are," Derek said, "about the sexiest woman alive."

Hearing him say that was like waking up after a long, troubled sleep. I smiled, and my whole body tingled. I didn't care if he had said that to a hundred women. He was saying it to *me*. I leaned into him, and with sure and practiced hands, he unzipped the back of my dress and let it slip to the floor. He caressed my face with more of his soft kisses, then he swooped me up and carried me to the bed. I was literally being swept off my feet … in a castle.

With a tender touch, Derek ran his fingertips across my bare stomach, sending shivers up and down my body. As we kissed, I undid the buttons of his shirt and trailed my hands across the muscular expanse of his chest, thrilled at every ripple, every curve, every dip. We lay there exploring each other's bodies before he finally undid the hook of my lacy bra. He cupped my breasts in his hands and kissed them gently, nearly sending me over the edge right then. I gripped his shoulders, digging my nails into his skin like one of the falcons in his care. He stopped and looked down at me.

"Don't stop," I murmured as I wrapped one leg around his waist.

He continued his kisses across my entire upper body. Just when I thought I couldn't take another second, he parted my legs and moved his face between them. I gasped for air as he delved into my most secret places with his tongue. I writhed around for what seemed like hours, sweating and dripping until I was spent.

"I'm not done with you yet," he said as he climbed on top of me.

I giggled softly in anticipation. He teased me for a bit, grinding against my pelvis at first, then touching me where I was smooth and wet. In the middle of his maddening kisses, Derek leaned over the side of the bed, fumbling with his pants. He unwrapped a condom and slid it on. With a guided thrust, he plunged into me. We rocked with a slow and steady rhythm, our bodies dancing to music only we could hear.

Derek lifted me off the bed, driving ever deeper. I locked my legs around him and let out a scream. He rocked against me and held me close. I sighed as the waves continued to roll inside me. Derek tensed up and shuddered, letting out his own primal howl.

We collapsed against the bed like two athletes, thoroughly exhausted and slick with sweat. In a few deep breaths, we fell asleep, but it wasn't long before we were reaching for each other again.

Derek left in the early daylight hours. I lay there in a blissful fog, listening to the birds chirping their incessant wake-up calls. More birds. Was that another sign? If so, what did it mean?

I rolled over and went back to sleep. I'd had enough omens for a while.

Chapter 9

HUNGER PANGS

When I woke later that morning, I thought I'd feel different, changed somehow. And for a few moments I did.

I ordered a pot of tea and ventured onto the balcony to take in the fresh air and revel in the dawn of a new day. I felt younger and prettier. More attractive than I'd felt in ages. My night with Derek had done wonders for my self-esteem. He got what all men want, but I got what I needed. He was *my* conquest, not the other way around. I didn't feel badly when he scampered out of bed at dawn. After all, there were rules and regulations about hotel employees fraternizing with guests. Or were there? Maybe he was just trying to get away from me.

By the time the tea arrived, I'd convinced myself he was off bragging to his friends about "shagging the American bird." I imagined Patrick and Daniel laughing over their morning chores as Derek regaled them with the story of how the night had unfurled, how he'd taken me to that "secret" spot on the lake where the staff seduced hotel guests after hours. They were all in on it. Patrick, Daniel, and Derek. They were birds of prey, circling the hotel grounds, and I was the timid creature snatched up in their talons. I had no more chance against them than the vermin they fed the birds at the falconry.

The idea of Derek as my conquest shriveled and slipped away. Familiar feelings of doubt, shame, and fear returned. I began to feel just as awful as I had when I got caught with Carson in Paso Robles. But I wasn't in California; I was in Ireland, and I wasn't betraying anyone. I didn't even have anyone to deceive anymore, except maybe myself. Still, I wanted to run. Away from Ashford Castle. Away from Ireland. I wanted to run to the airport and jump on the first flight home.

But I couldn't leave now. I'd finally made it to the county of my ancestors, and after more than a week in Ireland, I still hadn't been to see where my family came from. The place where one chapter ended and another began.

I took a sip of tea. The brew had gone cold, and I pushed it away. I'd promised myself, my mother, and my daughters that I'd learn as much as I could about our family history and bring the story back to California. I couldn't break that promise after only a week. So, I packed my bags and squeezed into my little Fiat, wedging my luggage behind the seat. I pointed the toy car in the direction of Westport and put Ashford Castle in the rearview mirror.

Westport wasn't far—no more than an hour according to the map. I drove along roads without shoulders, or even a line down the center, until I came to a sign that read "Cathair na Mart," the Irish name for Westport.

I felt better as soon as I pulled into the town. I'd driven through dozens of others, but Westport was one of the prettiest and most inviting I'd seen. I experienced a sensation of having been there before, similar to what I felt in Cong. I realized that many of the landmarks were familiar from stories Grandma Pat had told me over the years.

"In Westport, the Carrowbeg River runs through the center of town," she had told me, "with tree-lined promenades on either side. The streets have simple names like Bridge and Shop."

Just then, I found myself on Bridge Street, crossing the Carrowbeg River. In the distance, Croagh Patrick, a mountain that was the site of a famous annual pilgrimage, towered over the town. I was home!

As soon as I found a postcard, I would write to the women in my family and tell them about the idyllic town, with self-explanatory street names and a wide, flat river. It was an odd feeling to be so present, yet at the same time, so immersed in my past.

Though I had temporarily lost my connection to Grandma Pat at Ashford Castle, I regained it in Westport and instantly felt better about my night with Derek. It had been a wonderful evening, and there was no reason to think that he hadn't enjoyed it as much as I had. He probably had fond memories of his night in the castle with an American princess.

I went to the Heritage Centre, housed in a nineteenth-century stone building that wasn't much bigger than a truck. Inside, a polished table that looked like it had been there since the building was first constructed displayed information packets and brochures. Several chairs from the same time period were neatly arranged in a sitting area. I walked slowly through the room and took in the displays. The walls were hung with pictures of Ireland in the mid-1800s, sepia photos depicting the era of the Potato Famine. It looked like a museum in miniature.

A kind-looking woman stepped out from behind a worn wooden counter and greeted me. Her skin was free of freckles and anything but fair. Though she seemed much older than me, I could see past the strands of gray to know that her hair had once been as dark as mine.

"Can I help you?" she asked.

"I'm here to find my family," I said, which wasn't what I meant at all, but the woman seemed to know my intent.

"Of course you are."

She told me about the genealogy services offered by the Centre, and I agreed to the one that traced my family's history in the region. When I told her my maiden name, she looked up with a start.

"There's a McNally that runs a bed-and-breakfast here in town. Some of your people probably lived there before they emigrated to America."

We sat together around a low table. I pulled out a few photos of my ancestors (leaving the one of my naked grandmother tucked away) and went over some vague notes I had containing names and places that I believed were tied to my family history. The woman went to a file and began to fill out a chart for me. She promised to do some more research and gave me directions to the McNally B&B.

I thanked her, gathered up my things, and set off for the B&B. I had no trouble finding it. The cottage was old, weathered, and windowless. It looked resilient, defiant even. A simple thatched roof protected the two-hundred-year-old structure from western Ireland's persistent coastal rain. A man emerged from a half door and waved as I parked my car.

"Welcome," he said. "Me name's Connor McNally." He was thin with wiry, muscular arms. Brown curls spilled out from under his tweed cap.

"I'm a McNally, too," I said. "Barbara. From California. The woman down at the Heritage Centre recommended your place to me. Do you know her?"

"'Course," he said. Apparently, everyone knew everyone in Westport.

"So, McNally by way of California?" he asked.

"That's right," I said, taking the seat he offered. The top half of the single door remained open to the outside, latched to the whitewashed wall to let in light and fresh air.

A fire roared in the open fireplace, and pots and pans hung from pegs on the wall. Everything was so neat and tidy that I hardly noticed the floor was packed dirt. I imagined my ancestors sitting in that very spot, their feet touching the same ground. It was a dizzying thought. Aside from the occasional pop from the fireplace, the cottage was quiet, insulated from the sounds outside by its thick walls. As Connor talked, the warm, floury smell drifting over from the stove distracted me.

"Griddle bread?" he asked.

"I'd love some. I'm famished," I said and immediately regretted my choice of words. "I'm sorry."

"Don't be," he said. "An Gorta Mór—the Great Famine—is more than a memory in this part of the country. It's always with us. If ya're interested, there's a memorial up the road."

"I'd like to see it," I said and turned my attention to the bread and tea he set on the table. He took a seat next to me, bringing with him a crock of butter and a small pot of jam.

While I was hardly starving, I hadn't eaten all day.

"They give this to ya at the Heritage Centre?" Connor asked, indicating the preliminary genealogy report I'd laid on the table.

I nodded as I smeared a piece of hot griddle bread with butter and stuffed it into my mouth. The bread was soft, yet dense, and I could taste subtle hints of the soda that made it such an Irish treat. It tasted a lot like the griddle bread Grandma Pat used to make.

"Let's see what ya've got," he said. He reached for the chart and unfolded it in the dim light.

"Ah, yes. The McNallys. There are still plenty of us McNallys roaming around these parts. Our name means 'poor.' The clan is known as Black Irish because the native Irish mixed with Spanish survivors of the armada that wrecked off the coast of Westport. Lots of O'Dwyers around here, too. Their name means 'black' or 'dirt.' Some of us try not to live up to the roots of our names."

He took a closer look at the chart. "One woman in your bloodline is legendary—Grace O'Malley. Have you heard of her? She has quite a history here."

"Oh, my gosh. My grandmother used to tell me stories about her."

As I devoured more griddle bread and washed it down with hot tea, Connor told me about Gráinne Ní Mháille or Grace O'Malley, the Pirate Queen. Grace had been a strong-willed woman of means who lived in the area during the sixteenth century. Her family came from Clare Island, just off the coast of Westport, and she used it as a base of operations for her seafaring adventures. She attacked ships at sea and fortresses on the coast. A real take-no-prisoners kind of woman, admired for protecting Ireland. She was respected by men and women alike for her savvy techniques and recognized as a leader of fighting men, a real coup for a woman, especially in those days. Married several times to prominent figures, Grace accumulated a great deal of wealth, both through her own escapades and her inheritances. Grandma Pat had looked up to her as a kind of role model, a woman ahead of her time. A heroic warrior.

"My grandmother always described her as fearless."

Connor nodded. "She lived during a period of social change and political upheaval. From what I know, she ignored all the rules as to how a woman was supposed to act and became one of Ireland's foremost feminists."

I was intrigued by the possibility that our families were connected—that the blood of a pirate queen coursed through my veins. I imagined her with wild hair blowing in the sea breeze and bare-breasted like the figurehead of a ship—like Grandma Pat. A topless swashbuckler.

"What's so funny?" Connor asked.

I smiled and shook my head. "Are there are any portraits of Grace?"

"None that I know of, but there is a statue of her near Westport House, a historic home not far from here. Many books have been written about Grace O'Malley, and there have been a fair number of theatrical presentations and musicals depicting her," he said. "More bread?"

"Thank you, but no. I think I just gained ten pounds," I said, rubbing my stomach.

Our conversation turned to my family, and I told him how my great-great-grandmother, Bridget O'Dwyer, left for America during the Great Famine, which, I confessed, I didn't know much about.

Connor explained that a single fungus had ruined the potato crop, the main source of food for tenant farmers in the region. The men who worked the land didn't own it, but rented it from absentee landowners in England, who turned their backs on their tenants when the crop failed. After the blight, food was in such short supply that farmers and

their families starved. Their only choice was to turn to the
which accommodated as many as they could. But the poo
limited bed space and had to turn droves of people away. ____ who
couldn't find shelter were forced into the streets. The towns filled with
starving men, women, and children, who had no other option except to
leave Ireland. I felt a flash of guilt for my night with Derek. Grandma
Pat probably wouldn't have approved of me sleeping with the enemy,
so to speak.

Connor said things didn't get much better on the ships that took
people to America. In many cases, they were even worse. The crossing
was a grueling ordeal for most Irish men and women, who were forced
into steerage. It was not uncommon for two or three people to share
a bunk. And if one of them became sick, they all got sick. During
the exodus to America, many succumbed to typhoid, yellow fever,
or cholera. Thousands upon thousands died en route. Those that did
make it were often quarantined for long periods while they waited for
health inspectors to survey the ships, which they were often reluctant
to do. Many ships were turned away and sent to other ports. As a result,
someone who'd bought a ticket to New York or Boston would end up
in Baltimore or as far north as Canada, where they didn't know a soul.
They called them "coffin ships."

As Connor spoke, I thanked my great-great-grandmother for the
sacrifices she made for future generations of McNallys. Grandma Pat
had shared these stories with me many times over the years, but to be
sitting in the country of my ancestors, maybe even in a house that had
belonged to one of them, brought it all home. Bridget O'Dwyer was
one of eight girls. She was the only one brave enough to sail on a coffin
ship to America. Her sisters chose to stay in Ireland and either joined the
convent or starved to death. None of them had children. Suddenly, it all
seemed so real. Not a story. Not a legend. My relatives were real people
who endured real suffering. The griddle bread I'd greedily gobbled down
sat like a lead weight in my stomach.

"Excuse me, Connor," I said. "But I need to get some fresh air." The small, close room and the heat of the fire were making me feel light-headed.

Connor nodded. "I've a bicycle ya can use."

I dropped my bags in the back room of the tiny cottage, and Connor took me outside, where a cruiser with a wide, springy seat leaned against the wall. I rolled up my pants, threw a leg over the bicycle, and started pedaling. It had been years since I'd ridden a bike, and my spirits lifted almost immediately. I pedaled faster, wanting the bracing air on my face to blow away the troubled images that filled my head. I went down the lane toward the Octagon—a loop of pubs and shops in the center of town near the massive statue of Saint Patrick. A few pedestrians walked the streets, carrying paper sacks from the shops in town back to their homes. I made my way west, around the bay, and toward the mountain that cast its shadow over Westport.

I soon found myself out in the open, surrounded by inlets and waterways. A soft mist hung over the water, and it appeared as if it might rain at any moment. As in Dingle, I passed Celtic crosses and roved past fields full of sheep, their shaggy coats heavy with moisture. I didn't know which road to take, but it hardly seemed to matter. I let the dark slopes of Croagh Patrick be my guide.

I started thinking about Derek. He wasn't some kid looking for a good time, but a man in his thirties trying to make a better life for himself. During dinner he'd told me about the classes he was taking part-time in order to finish school. Yes, having sex with Derek was impulsive, but so was storming out of the castle like a woman with her honor besmirched. Leaving might have been the more impulsive of the two acts. A satisfied pirate queen wouldn't have given Derek a second thought.

But I did. I'd thought about him quite a bit that day. Sometimes I disparaged myself for having sex with him, and sometimes I felt badly for leaving like I did, without saying good-bye. Either way, I felt guilty.

I imagined a disappointed Derek ringing my room and being told that I'd already checked out. Then I imagined a triumphant Derek boasting of his night in the castle to his coworkers at the falconry. I attributed my guilt, in part, to the conservative Baptist environment in which I was raised. Sex was a woman's duty—it was her responsibility to please her husband. Women weren't supposed to have sex for fun.

Even though I had been exploring the boundaries of my upbringing for some time, my night with Derek weighed heavily on me. Finally, I decided just to let it go. It was a fling. I had no expectations and no obligations. In all likelihood, I would never see Derek again. Besides, I didn't come to Ireland to find love; I came to find my ancestors, my roots, my soul.

As I pedaled toward Croagh Patrick, I came to a sign for the National Famine Memorial and made the turn. As I approached the memorial, a bronze ship becalmed in a sea of concrete, I let out a startled gasp. What I first thought were tattered sails hanging from the masts were instead haunting representations of the dead, twisted in the rigging. Hollow skulls and outstretched bones, skeletons aboard the ship, bore tribute to those who had suffered and died or emigrated during the Great Famine.

Alone at the monument, I parked the bicycle and walked around the massive sculpture. The prevailing wind blew in from the west, and the skeletons seemed to be hanging on for dear life, even in death. Not for the first time, I wondered what I would have done if I'd been in their situation. Would I have had the courage to leave? To stare down death and disease and make a new life for myself in a country I didn't know? No car. No grocery store. No credit cards.

I sat in the grass at the base of the looming black sculpture. The empty eye sockets of the tormented skeletons filled me with anguish until all I could do was drop my head and cry. I don't know if it was anxiety left over from the morning's hasty departure or if I was spent from all of the running around I'd been doing, but the thought of fellow human beings—and relatives—stuck in those rank coffin ships overwhelmed me. I cried for my great-great-grandmother, Bridget. I cried for Grandma Pat. I cried for my mother. I cried for myself. I even cried for Grace, the Pirate Queen. The life of a pirate couldn't have been easy. If only she'd been alive during the Great Famine. I imagined her saving thousands of lives and rewriting history.

When I thought I was all cried out, I reflected on my daughters and how I had broken our family into wounded fragments, how I had crushed the pieces so that they would never fit back together again. The tears continued to flow, and I cried until I had nothing left.

A chill hung in the air and rain clouds swept over Clew Bay. Sitting in the shadow of the monument, I took a few deep breaths and tried to regain my composure. My divorce was not an act of failure. It was one of liberation. I hoped that one day my daughters would understand this.

I'd set out on my jaunt toward Croagh Patrick with the thought of climbing the mountain and paying my respects to Ireland's patron saint as thousands did every summer, but the National Famine Monument had left me drained. I was done with saints. I'd walk a mountain for Grace, but old Saint Pat would have to find another supplicant. What I really wanted was a cold beer and some hot food. I wanted to be around people, not skeletons and crumbling statuary.

Chapter 10

UNIONS AND REUNIONS

I pedaled back into town and found a pub with a window where I could keep an eye on Connor's bicycle. It being a Saturday, the pub was full of people enjoying the day. A fiddler scratched out some tunes and a mandolin player sang Irish ballads. Old men sat at the tables, sipping their healers. Kids darted between video games, trying to make the buttons and joysticks work without the required coins. In the corner of the room, the television screen broadcast a soccer match from somewhere in South America, but nobody seemed to be paying attention. My stomach rumbled with hunger after my emotional trip to the monument, so I ordered a pint of Guinness and a bowl of fisherman's stew.

The stew arrived, smelling of the sea. The light-colored broth was flecked with bits of thyme and thickened with chunks of white fish and new potatoes. Diced onions and kernels of corn peeked from below the steaming surface, and as I took my first bite, I smelled a hint of garlic. The next thing I knew, I had company. A fellow who introduced himself as Jack sat down next to me. Deep lines crossed his broad forehead, exposed by the receding hairline of his wiry gray locks. His cheeks bore the flush of a man who spent too much time in pubs.

"Ya haven't been to the National Famine Memorial have ya?"

"Yes, I was just there."

"Jaysus, ya Americans are morbid. Ya like jokes?"

"Sure."

"If ya had a penis growing out of your yer forehead, how big would it be?"

I nearly spit up my stew. "I don't know."

"And ya never would," shouted Jack. "Because yer bollocks would be hanging down in front of yer eyes."

I laughed and accepted his offer of another pint. If need be, I could walk the bike back to Connor's. Jack took it as an invitation to continue flirting.

"Is a quick seventh-degree union out of the question?"

"I'm not sure," I said. "What is it?"

Jack explained how back in the Dark Ages of Ireland, there were ten levels of marriage. The seventh-degree union was also called a soldier's union: a one-night stand.

"Seven is me lucky number," he said with a wink.

"Not today it isn't," I said, winking back.

It was Jack's turn to laugh.

"Maybe the Dark Ages were really the Enlightened Ages," I said.

Jack nodded. "In Ireland, marriage has only one form—insoluble." He took a long draw of his Guinness, swilling it down as if it were water.

"I thought divorce was legal now."

"Aye, since 1995. But ya have to be separated for four years before ya can even file." Jack's chair screeched loudly on the floor as he scooted a little closer to me. I nudged my own chair a little further away and studied my stew.

My uncontested divorce took only nine months. I couldn't imagine the toll it would have taken on my daughters if the battle had lasted four years.

"So ya better not pick a pig's arse for yer mate, because ya'll be stuck with him for all eternity." He drew the back of his sleeve across his mouth to wipe away the foam left behind by his last gulp of Guinness.

"Or her," I added.

Then I asked him about the ring he wore on his left hand, where a traditional wedding band would go.

"This is a Claddagh ring. Have you not seen 'em?" I shook my head, and Jack continued.

"It gets its name from a fishing village just outside Galway." He leaned over the table to show me the ring. "The heart is held by two hands, with a crown on top. The hands mean friendship, the crown means loyalty, and the heart, as everybody knows, means love."

"Friendship, loyalty, love," I echoed.

"That's it, missy. Wearing the ring with the heart facing out means ya're free for the picking. Wearing the heart facing inward means ya're not." Jack's ring faced in.

"Maybe I need one of those rings to let the world know I'm single."

"As long as ya're the one that knows, that's all that matters."

Did I know? I seemed to be caught in a state of limbo. I wasn't married anymore, but I wasn't free either. Everywhere I went, I dragged my baggage with me. Homemaker turned home wrecker. Impulsive, yet guilt-ridden. Lonely divorcée. Uncomfortable in her own skin. What a combination. What a mess.

My emotions got the best of me. The music faded as my eyes welled up. Jack put his hand over mine and gave it a fatherly squeeze, as if he knew exactly how I felt.

"Now that I see which way your ring is facing," I said, "I believe you were joking about a union."

"Aye," he said, cracking a rueful smile, "but not all jokes are funny."

———※———

After a proper Irish breakfast by the fire, I borrowed Connor's bike again. The morning was full sunshine for a change, and I wanted to visit the graveyard in Aughavel to see if I could find any of my relatives. Maybe Jack at the pub had been right about me after all. Maybe I was morbid. But I didn't see it that way. I wanted to pay my respects to my ancestors and keep their memories alive.

Aughavel was on the outskirts of town. I pedaled over the cobblestone roads past the Poorhouse, a historical site where the impoverished had been left to die when they could no longer pay their debts. I didn't stop. It seemed like a place where I'd get angry and upset all over again at the injustice of it all. Across the street from the Poorhouse was a large pit that Connor had told me about where the dead were thrown for their final rest. No memorial had ever been erected there. It seemed some places were too sad, even for the Irish.

I hadn't expected my visit to Westport to be so emotional. I had known that my ancestors had suffered, but visiting the monument and cycling past the Poorhouse and the nearby pit made my insides hurt. Most Americans, living in the land of dreams, were oblivious to this kind of suffering. I was no different. I'd been blind to the significance of my ancestors' suffering until I walked that same path, pedaled that same road.

The cemetery at Aughavel was different from American cemeteries— the burial grounds were much smaller and, obviously, considerably older. The dead were packed closely together without any spaces between the plots or a path to guide me. It felt disrespectful walking on top of the graves, but I didn't have a choice. I took small steps, and silly as it sounds, tried to tread lightly. The sun had heated up the soil, and it smelled like peat and mulch. I walked across the spongy grass, looking for my ancestors' names on the ivy- and moss-covered headstones. Time had washed away many of the inscriptions, some of which had been there long before the United States was a country.

I knelt down in front of a smooth, white headstone, reaching out to trace the letters: "Skepticism is the beginning of faith." That was worth remembering. I reached inside my pocket and took out a notepad so I could record the epitaph and take it home with me. I rose up and searched for something else I could read. When I found another legible one, I had to stop and think. "May you live all the days of your life." At first it seemed trivial and obvious, but then I thought about it in the context of living, really living, and it all made sense. I added it to my notepad.

I found McNallys, O'Dwyers, and O'Malleys dating back to 1850, but those names were so common that it was impossible to know if they were my ancestors. I scrawled what I could read of the names and dates into my notepad to bring back to the woman at the Heritage Centre. I hoped my ancestors were there at Aughavel and not in the mass burial pit in town.

Walking across the bones of the dead, I felt truly mortal. I understood that no matter what happened in this life, I, too, was going to die. Not necessarily soon, but someday. I didn't know what waited for me on the other side. My parents probably thought I would join Grandma Pat in hell. Their church taught religious beliefs as if they were immutable facts. But the past year had taught me that life was not so black-and-white. There were gray areas that blurred the boundaries between beliefs and religions, between right and wrong. The time I spent with Fiona at the Celtic service and speaking with Wiccans had given me an understanding of a universe much more in keeping with my feelings about life, though that hardly made the notion of death bearable. I stood in that place thinking that no matter how far I traveled or how long I ran, death would someday catch up to me.

For a moment, I felt the appeal of believing in the life after death that my childhood church taught. With a little work, I could probably put myself back on the track to heaven. I even thought about giving reincarnation a shot so I could come back as a pirate queen like Grace O'Malley. Then I saw Grandma Pat shaking her head in disapproval. To her, so much of religion was putting off to the next world what one ought to be doing in this one. "You only have one life to live," she'd often said.

It always sounded like a corny platitude. It was the name of a soap opera, after all. But standing in an ancient cemetery in a wild place hammered the point home. I had always thought of a cemetery as orderly and efficient, a place where things were clearly marked, the beginnings and endings etched in stone for all to see. But the worn-off names and dates made me realize that nothing lasts forever. My great-great-grandmother was brave. She was a survivor. I wanted to carry her in my heart along with Grandma Pat and live my life the way they did: as a mother, lover, fighter, sage.

It felt as if Grandma Pat spoke in my ear. *Live today fully and embrace it with joy. Tomorrow and the hereafter will take care of themselves.* I could hear her encouraging me to let go of my resentments from the past. There was no need to carry any of that with me. Life was too short. There simply wasn't any time.

I took out the photo of naked Grandma Pat and placed it on a gravestone that had no name on it, a crooked slab that had begun its inexorable journey underground. Kneeling, I felt moisture from the damp earth seep through my jeans. The day before, I'd cried for all the women in my family. There at Aughavel, I bowed my head and thanked them for their sacrifices.

I thanked Grace O'Malley for her spirit. I thanked my great-great-grandmother, Bridget, for her courage and fortitude. I thanked Grandma Pat for her wisdom. I imagined my female ancestors and Grace O'Malley linked arm in arm, watching over me. Turning my face toward the bright noon sun, I sent a beam of affirmation to the heavens.

Since I had arrived in Ireland, my understanding of life and religion had been ripped open and exposed, and there in Aughavel, I felt as if it had been sown back together. I still didn't know exactly what I believed, but I was at peace knowing that I came from brave, honest stock. I had the genes to be a strong, independent woman, to do good things in life. Rising, I knew I was ready to go back to California. My time in Ireland was over.

Chapter 11

TEA WITH SISTER
I'M-OKAY-WITH-THAT

I had one more day before my flight back to California, so I went to explore the history of the village of Knock in County Mayo. There, on August 21, 1879, three holy figures appeared outside the Knock Parish Church; fifteen people witnessed an apparition of the Virgin Mary, Saint John the Evangelist, and Saint Joseph. Soon Knock, with one-and-a-half million visitors each year, found itself on par with Fatima and Lourdes. Its status as a Marian Shrine got a boost one hundred years after the apparition when Pope John Paul II paid a visit. In 1993, Mother Teresa of Calcutta visited. So many people made the pilgrimage to the parish church, rechristened the Church of the Apparition, that the grounds were expanded to a sprawling complex, including a massive modern basilica—the first in Ireland. The tiny town of fewer than a thousand souls even gained an international airport.

I reached Knock in less than an hour driving east from Westport under blue skies laced with billowing clouds. The streets teemed with vendors hawking holy water, figurines, and other trinkets. It reminded me of the New Testament money changers, milling around the temple. Some had set up portable kiosks, while others wore their wares around their neck, holding out samples to everyone who passed by. The throngs of people who'd come on their pilgrimages to honor Our Lady of Knock were intent on bringing home souvenirs. They seemed to be taking away more than just their purchases. Their faces glowed with serenity, so maybe they knew something I didn't.

Knock was not at all what I expected. The church complex almost looked more American than Irish, more modern than historic, a stark contrast to the countryside filled with ancient ruins. The Church of the Apparition was an old stone structure, but it had a glassed-in extension to the rear, where the apparition was first seen. The enclosed area allowed pilgrims inside to view replicas of the apparition in a protected environment, bathed in natural light, while the glass walls allowed visitors to view the statues from the outside, looking in. A basilica with an enormous Space Needle of a steeple dominated the grounds, and a huge Celtic cross, erected in honor of Pope John II's visit, towered high above the other structures. Little trams shuttled weary visitors between the buildings.

I examined the statues depicting Mary, John, and Joseph as they were said to have appeared. Mary stood center stage, swathed in a long stone robe that fastened at her neck. She was tall and thin, with her hands parted and raised slightly. Beneath a large gold crown, her eyes looked toward the heavens. On Mary's left, Saint John the Evangelist held an open book in his left arm, his robe draped in deep folds across his chest. His right arm was raised high, and he looked as if he were preaching. An older-looking, bearded Saint Joseph stood to the right of the Virgin Mary with his head bowed toward her.

The three statues looked holy and ethereal. Lifelike, yet surreal. I wrestled with the reality of the apparition. Since all those people saw it at the same time, it must have happened, right? But the skeptic in me wondered how those people all knew they were looking at the Virgin Mary, Saint John the Evangelist, and Saint Joseph without exchanging any words. Did they just know? Was that true faith? I wished I could believe like that, but something always held me back.

I entered the basilica, where mass was in progress, and instantly felt the sanctified air of ritual. A reverent hush filled the stadium-sized sanctuary, broken only by the priest's lilting voice, which echoed off the soaring ceiling as he recited the mass. It was peak season, and the pews inside were filled with pilgrims and tourists alike, asking absolution and seeking miracles. I slipped into an empty spot in the back and studied the painted murals depicting Jesus on the cross and angels floating in the clouds.

In the vaulted worship chambers, I soon found myself entranced more by the atmosphere of the basilica than the words of the priest. He caught my attention when he began to pray to the Virgin Mary, reciting the Perpetual Novena to Our Lady of Knock. I followed along with the leaflet in the pew.

"Our Lady of Knock, Queen of Ireland, you gave hope to your people in a time of distress and comforted them in sorrow. You've inspired countless pilgrims to pray with confidence to your divine Son, remembering His promise, 'Ask and ye shall receive, seek and ye shall find.'"

Praying to the Virgin Mary was new to me. I'd been raised to believe that she was a false god. But staring up at her statue, I felt something different. First and foremost, Mary was a mother. *The* mother. A mother who'd lost her son. Catholics and non-Catholics alike believed Jesus took the form of man when on earth; yet he chose to come into the world through a woman. That underscored Mary as a symbol of a life-giving force. By venerating Mary, a woman and a mother, we were honoring all women. But why did she have to be a virgin? Did that mean sex was bad?

My mother never broached the topic of sex with her three girls. It simply wasn't discussed. In our world, sex was for bad girls. Good girls didn't talk about sex because it would be tantamount to admitting they'd had it, which was a sin. I struggled over the contradiction of the Virgin Mary and her motherhood. Was one better than the other? Did those who worshipped her strive to model themselves after her purity or her maternity?

Once the service was over, I lingered in the sanctuary. Shafts of sunlight pierced the enormous stained-glass windows. Surrounded by the smell of incense and the flicker of candles, I mused about the Catholic Church, plagued by scandals involving priests who sexually abused thousands of children. I couldn't help but wonder about the robed priest who'd just finished reciting mass—was he one of them?

A cheeky grin crossed my face. I was in one of the holiest places in all of Ireland, and I kept thinking about whether the priest kept his pecker in his pants! In my mind, it went against the laws of human nature to ask men to clamp down their sexual energy and take a vow of celibacy. Was it any wonder those frustrated priests unleashed their unfulfilled urges in deviant ways? The manner in which they abused their power over children to relieve their selfish needs was a tragic reality. My smirk turned to sadness as I contemplated a situation that seemingly had no solution.

Sex was meant to augment a healthy relationship. When sex was no longer a mutual bonding experience in my marriage, I made it an adulterous pleasure. As a single divorcée, I was free to express the dimensions of myself that I'd been reluctant to explore in my marriage. Carson and Derek had shown me that I could experience my sexuality in an exhilarating way, but I needed to reconcile my spirituality with my sexuality without jumping into bed with the first man who smelled like hay.

Rising to leave the church, I eased out of the pew, but when I turned, I ran smack into a nun. Of all the people attending mass that day, I had to plow into a nun. She wore a crisp black-and-white habit that hid everything except her face. Still, I could see that she was frail and elderly. Her skin fell in soft folds of pale translucence. Her back hunched with age.

"Oh, my goodness! I'm so sorry!"

"'Tis all right, child. Take more than a wisp like yerself to knock me down. Did ya enjoy the service?"

"Oh, yes. It was beautiful," I said, even though the service had left me confused about Mary and the complicated relationship between sexuality and spirituality.

"Where do ya come from?" The nun looked at me intently, her eyes dark and focused beneath drooping eyelids.

"The States," I said. "California."

"Well, welcome to God's country. Would ya care to join me for a spot of tea? I was just heading to the hospitality house to put on the kettle."

I was taken aback by the nun's invitation. It seemed odd that she would invite a stranger, a foreigner, to tea just because their paths crossed in the sanctuary. But maybe this was yet another serendipitous stroke of luck. Maybe the nun had a message that I needed to hear.

"That would be grand," I said. "If you think it's okay. I was raised a Baptist." I'd never met a nun before, and I wasn't sure if she was allowed to socialize with people from other religions.

"Follow me. I am part of the Saint Mary of the Angels order here in Knock. We welcome all religions."

She walked slowly but resolutely across the grassy complex toward a small stone house with pointed gables and two tall chimneys. As we walked, she introduced herself as Sister Catherine and said she'd been with the order for almost sixty years.

I suddenly felt embarrassed. What if she asked me if I was married? What would I say? Yes, but I ran off with a horse whisperer? Sister Catherine and I came from such different worlds. I had been married for twenty-three years, had extramarital affairs, and just romped my way through a passionate one-night stand. She had never even had sex.

As we approached the hospitality house, Sister Catherine opened the massive front door with a practiced tug and led me through the foyer to a dimly lit kitchen. In the center of the room, a glass vase with a single rose sat atop a wooden table.

Sister Catherine pulled out a chair and gestured for me to sit while she filled the electric kettle with water and set two chipped, tea-stained cups on the table. Each china cup, decorated with a delicate floral pattern, rested on a matching saucer.

"So, ya were raised a Baptist," she said. "What brought ya to us today?"

"I guess you could say I'm on a bit of a spiritual journey." I looked around the kitchen. Mounted to the wall across from the table, a small statue of the Virgin Mary watched over us.

"Well, nothing wrong with that. We find God in mysterious ways."

"Yes, but ..." I hesitated. "Doesn't that go against your faith? I mean, exploring different ideas?" The water started to boil with a muted echo, rolling rhythmically inside the electric kettle. Sister Catherine filled a stout teapot with the hot water and set it aside to steep.

"Oh, dear me, child, the church is my calling, and I believe in its teachings, but 'tis the exploration of new ways of thinking that enhances and enriches my beliefs. If ya ask me, I believe that religion has become too political. The next evolution is to tear down our walls so that we can see God in everyone. It will take some time, but I'm okay with that. Maybe someday Christianity will actually be practiced."

Sister Catherine seemed rather progressive for an old Irish nun. While she cut us each a slice of seed cake and filled our cups with tea, I asked her how she decided to become a sister. She told me it was the desire to serve others and the joy it brought her that made her join. In her sixty years at the convent, she had taken on many tasks and now worked as a counselor. She said she loved the nurturing aspects of being a nun and the opportunities to meet interesting people.

"Do you ever feel like you missed anything?" I asked, nibbling on my cake. The caraway seeds crunched between my teeth.

She laughed. "Perhaps, but I have gained wisdom and experiences that I never would have found in the outside world."

"Do you regret not having children?" I sipped my tea.

"I'll admit that when I first joined the order, I felt a twinge or two about it, but I believed I had a higher calling. Truth be told, there is a part of me that hopes the Catholic Church will someday allow women who take the vow to be mothers."

"Do you think it could happen?" The front door opened, and I caught a glimpse of another nun, who passed wordlessly by the kitchen on her way to another part of the hospitality house. Her starched robe swished across the floor as she strode into the recesses of the old building.

"Why not? As for me, though my body may not have been a vessel, I feel as though I have been given the gift of motherhood by working with the young sisters who come into the order. Over the years, I have built wonderful bonds with so many young women. I believe ya can be maternal without giving birth."

"So Mary represents the nurturing quality of a woman, whether or not she chooses to give birth?"

"All women have a feminine side that includes maternal nurturing, though some may be better than others at showing it."

Wasn't that the truth! So many women who had children were ill equipped to handle them, while others who never had children were incredibly nurturing and kind. But wouldn't someone with maternal gifts feel the loss of sexual intimacy more acutely? Sister Catherine would know. I stared at the crumbs on my plate, debating whether I should probe a little deeper. I felt at ease with her, as if I could ask her anything. So I did—sort of.

"Do you ever wonder, what it would have been like, to ... you know ..." I let my voice trail off.

"Be a mother?"

"Have sex," I whispered.

"Well, dear, I can't say I'm all that familiar with the practice." Sister Catherine shifted in her chair, and it creaked beneath her weight.

"I'm sorry. I didn't mean to make you uncomfortable." I hadn't really intended to ask a nun about sex, but my visit to Knock had raised some heated questions in my mind.

"Not at all," she said, a glimmer in her eyes. "I enjoy the male energy, but as a nun, exploring that energy is forbidden. As a woman, I often consider that untouched part of me. What woman wouldn't? But pleasing myself simply for self-gratification would be selfish."

Wasn't that like saying it was selfish to eat ice cream because it tastes so good? Maybe she hid her sexuality because she had to. Was it possible she covertly recognized it and permitted herself the occasional indulgence? If so, that was a small sin, considering what she was sacrificing in the name of God.

"When I joined the order," she continued, "I thought about my commitment in terms of directing my energy toward the pursuit of the spiritual. If I were going into the order today, I might feel differently." She poured us each more tea.

"But is it possible to travel down both roads: the spiritual and the sexual?"

"Of course," Sister Catherine replied. "There's not a one of us who doesn't have both of those things in us. We're Christ-like in that we are spiritual beings with physical bodies."

"So, the blending of the spiritual with the carnal makes sense to you?" I asked. "I'm learning that spirituality and sexuality aren't separate. I grew up in a conservative Baptist home where the two didn't mix, and now in Ireland, I've encountered spiritual Wiccans, who honor sensuality, and men who are interested in my soul, not just my body."

"The more fully human we are, dear, the more God-like we become. I think ya have to celebrate yer sexuality for those who can't openly do the same."

"You remind me of my grandmother," I said.

"I'll take that as a compliment." With a wan smile, Sister Catherine smoothed her tunic over her legs.

Mother, lover, fighter, sage. Like Grandma Pat, I couldn't live a one-dimensional life—or even two. There was so much more. My patriarchal upbringing and marriage had encouraged only the aspects of mother and, perhaps, sage. At least from the male point of view. I wanted to embrace the lover and the fighter, too. I wanted to be passionate and stand up for what I believed. The Wiccans had shown me the value and power of the feminine warrior within. The pirate queen, my ancestors, Grandma Pat, and even Sister Catherine had shown me that it was perfectly acceptable, maybe even commendable, to have and enjoy sex, to speak up for what I wanted.

"Since we're talking about sex ..."

"Oh, dear." Sister Catherine glanced around the room as if to be certain that no one was eavesdropping on our unconventional conversation. She reached up to adjust her habit, then folded her hands in her lap.

"I was thinking about Mary today and wondered why she had to be a virgin when she gave birth to Jesus. Couldn't she have been a regular mom who already had kids?"

"That's a good question. Many abandon their faith because of it—especially women. I've thought about it, too, of course, but it's not for me to decide. It was God's will."

So Sister Catherine was wise, but she didn't have all the answers. As we finished our tea, a group of sisters strolled quietly through the kitchen. Sister Catherine nodded at them and chuckled softly.

"See, we still wear our habits even though we haven't had to since 1965. Change is hard."

When we finished our tea, I thanked Sister Catherine for her time, and she gave me a hug that belied her small stature.

"Safe travels on the rest of yer journey," she said. "Wherever it is ya're trying to go."

As I drove away from Knock, I was struck by the synchronicity of my meeting with Sister Catherine and her willingness to answer my questions. Sister Catherine reminded me of Grandma Pat in so many ways. On the surface, they couldn't have been more different, but they were both women of strong convictions and inquisitive minds. Sister Catherine had inspired me to be less judgmental, but our talk left me feeling a little sad, too. I could envision her doting on her grandkids or going dancing with Grandma Pat, but the regimented life that Sister Catherine led seemed destined to die off with the aging sisters. Where will they find young women to keep the faith and the order alive?

On my way to the airport, I felt a sense of resolution. I was a McNally through and through. I liked seeking new adventures, and sex was a part of that. But as much as I held Grandma Pat up as a role model, I was never going to be the brassy, boisterous life-of-the-party that she was. I enjoyed doing things for others and cared about what others thought about me. In that way, I was more like my mother. Each of those aspects was a vital part of me. They had helped me build a career, even if I'd abandoned it, and they would help me again in my new life. I wasn't going to suppress parts of my personality to make a relationship work anymore.

I didn't have to change. I realized that I just had to be myself. Barbara. My flaws were part of my character, and I was learning to love myself. It wasn't easy. I was headed home, but in my heart I knew my journey wasn't over.

Chapter 12

FIFTY GOLDEN YEARS

When I returned to California, I imagined the sins of my past bundled up and spinning around and around, unclaimed on an empty carousel at Shannon Airport. I wasn't the same clueless person who had jumped on the jet to Ireland. I came back more aware of myself and of my place in the world, more confident and less dependent. I'd made mistakes, and I'd make more, but I was willing to take responsibility for my actions. That didn't mean I had to shoulder the blame for everything that had gone wrong. Nor was I obligated to carry that load for the rest of my life. Ireland taught me to move on and leave the baggage behind.

My girls picked me up at LAX on the day of my parents' fiftieth wedding anniversary. We exchanged hugs, and I held them at arm's length, certain they looked like they had grown up while I was away. Little things like the way Kelly wore her hair and the stylish handbag Molly swung over her shoulder made them seem more mature. I wondered if they sensed any difference in me.

"Wanna drive?" Molly asked, handing me the keys.

"Sure!" I said and started for the passenger door.

"Welcome home, Mom," Kelly said. "Just in case you forgot, the driver sits on the left here."

I walked around to the correct side and started up the car. The congested slab of the 405 stretched out for more lanes than I could count, and I longed for the narrow Irish roads, even with their silly roundabouts. Back in California, everything seemed to be covered in asphalt or made out of concrete. Sure, the sun was shining, but the green fields and misty forests of Ireland felt as if they were a million miles away. Was this what people meant when they referred to "reentry syndrome"?

My parents' suburban backyard seemed like a fitting party venue for a couple that didn't like to make a fuss and seldom, if ever, strayed from the path of comfortable conformity. Each of the cookie-cutter houses in their planned community looked the same from the outside. Like the others, my parents' yard was tastefully manicured, with a smooth green lawn and roses in full bloom.

A silver banner stretched across the garage door with the words "Happy 50th Anniversary" set in multicolored letters. As Molly and Kelly scrambled out of the car, I sat behind the wheel for a moment. It was the first social function I had attended with my family and all their friends since my divorce was finalized six months earlier. My two sisters would be there with their families, too. Someone was bound to say something. My mother would probably pounce on the opportunity to express her disappointment in me.

"You can do this, Barbara," I said aloud as I got out of the car to join the girls.

The tension built in my neck and shoulders as we walked up the red brick pathway. It was as if I already could feel my parents' judgment pressing down on me. My father was an old-fashioned traditionalist, and my mother was subdued and subservient. They believed in the institution of marriage and always seemed happy in their reserved relationship, while I had dishonored my family with the scandal of divorce. I was the black sheep, the one who couldn't figure out how to make my marriage work.

The stifling lemon scent of rigorously polished furniture assaulted our senses as soon as we stepped inside. The living room was carefully appointed with decorator sets straight from the showroom floor. The three of us hurried through the sterile kitchen, eager to get outside where the air was fresh. The backyard was dotted with circular tables, each draped with a crisp white tablecloth and adorned with a small bowl of roses.

I didn't recognize any of the guests chatting on the patio, so no one slowed us down as we went in search of my parents. I spotted Dad entertaining in one corner, Mom in another. It seemed odd that my parents would celebrate their fiftieth anniversary separately. Maybe that was their secret to a happy marriage.

"Grandma sure went all out on this one," Kelly said as she grabbed a Coke from a cooler.

"Well, fifty years is a pretty big deal," Molly said. She pulled a tube of lipstick and a compact mirror from her purse, then painted her lips a subtle shade of pink with practiced ease.

"Yeah, I guess it is," said Kelly. I could hear the pain of my divorce resurfacing in her voice.

My shoulders sagged. I didn't have to look at Kelly to feel her sadness. The long shadow of my actions lingered in my daughters' lives. I may have moved on, but they clearly hadn't yet. They might not ever get over it. The best I could hope for was a trace of enlightenment—that if, God forbid, they were ever unhappy in a job or marriage it was better to leave than to live a lie, regardless of what others might say.

Kelly toyed with the pop-top on her Coke before opening it. Molly shifted her weight from one foot to the other and looked uneasily around the yard. I sensed the anxiety in both of them.

"What's going on?" I asked.

"Dad got remarried," Kelly blurted. She held her Coke with both hands, as if steadying the drink would calm her nerves.

"Are you kidding me?" I nearly shouted. "When?"

"No joke, Mom. It just happened, while you were in Ireland," Molly said, filling in at least one of the blanks.

Kelly set down her Coke and fumbled for her phone. "I have a picture."

While she searched for the phone, I waited for the news to sink in. But it didn't sink. It crashed. My stomach churned into an uncomfortable knot, and my throat grew tight.

So they went to the wedding? Of course they did—he was their father. But still, that stung. It felt like a betrayal, which was ridiculous. I was the betrayer. Did I even want to know the details of the event?

"Here," Kelly said, handing me the phone with a full-screen photo. I didn't want to look at it. I needed a drink, a place to sit, and a hole to disappear into. I glanced at the photo, afraid of what I'd see.

The photo filled in another blank. Jay's new wife was his old college sweetheart. The one before me. He didn't waste any time, did he? She must have been waiting in the wings all along. It was all so ridiculous that I whooped with laughter.

"Mom?" Molly asked. "Are you okay? You look—"

"Relieved," I said, forcing a smile and taking a deep breath.

"Really?" the girls said in unison. My doubting daughters. Kelly looked from me to her older sister and back to me with a confused expression. At eighteen and twenty-two, they must have had a hard time trying to make sense of it all.

"This means he's moved on," I said as I returned the phone to her. "I don't have to feel like I screwed up his life anymore."

Molly and Kelly looked at one another again, somehow sensing that I didn't need to know the details of the wedding.

"Well, now that door is closed once and for all, and I can move on, too. And hey—at least she's not some twenty-five-year-old twit."

"Mom!" The girls laughed at my brash dismissal of Jay's new wife, and we relaxed into a comfortable group of three, not a divided contingent of two-against-one.

"No offense. Now put that phone away. Here comes your grandmother."

My mom approached, seeming more vivacious than usual. She greeted us with a cheery smile that matched her bright pink pantsuit. As she hugged Molly, then Kelly, I was startled by how much she reminded me of Grandma Pat. Usually she struck me as just the opposite, but that day she was radiant, confident, and even sassy—much like her own mother.

"I invited my grandchildren without checking with you, Barbara," she said. "I didn't know you were back, and frankly, even if I had known, I wouldn't have expected you to come."

She acted just as cold as I had anticipated. My failed marriage had opened a broad gap between my family and me, and we hadn't connected much lately.

"Come, girls. Dinner is starting." She put her arms around Molly and Kelly and drew them in, away from me, before shuttling them off to her friends.

Nice to see you, too, Mother, I thought as I wishfully scanned the party for a waiter or waitress ferrying cocktails. But no such luck at a conservative Christian party. One drink wasn't going to cut it, anyway. I would want to grab the whole tray.

I found my two sisters, Brea and Mary, and exchanged superficial pleasantries with them before choosing a solitary seat in the back corner of the yard, near the bougainvillea climbing the rear fence. Dad's booming voice called the guests to dinner, a presentation of gleaming white plates piled with fragrant filet mignon, whipped potatoes, and buttery strands of green beans topped with slivered almonds. Murmurs of appreciation came from every table. The perfect dinner, the perfect party, the perfect couple. Slumped alone in my corner of the yard, I could barely keep my eyes open as the jet lag I'd been fighting off finally set in.

It seemed like hours before champagne was poured. My parents were still stiff, but they had loosened up ever so slightly since my youth, indulging in the occasional glass of wine. The celebratory bubbles were accompanied by cheesecake smothered in strawberries. "Oohs!" and "aahs!" filtered through the evening air. My older sister stood up from her seat near the patio and loudly clinked her knife against her glass.

"Excuse me. Excuse me!" Brea called above the din.

Her snow-white décolletage contrasted sharply with her off-the-shoulder black dress. Even from across the yard, I could see her hardware glimmering in the setting sun: a multicarat diamond necklace and set of matching earrings. She cleared her throat and fingered the stem of her glass.

"I just wanted to thank everyone for being here this evening to celebrate with my mom and dad—fifty years of wedded bliss." She paused to allow the crowd to burst into enthusiastic applause, then she smiled and resumed talking. "I don't know too many kids who are as lucky as we are. My sisters and I had such an extraordinary childhood. Stand up here with me, girls. Come on over!"

The guests scanned the yard, looking for the two sisters who would complete the trio. Mary quickly rose and joined Brea at her table. When I tried to get up, my legs almost gave way. I stood for a moment, grasping the edge of the table, then slowly walked over to join my siblings, feeling like a party crasher.

"Our father made sure we had a great roof over our heads," Brea continued, "and our mother saw to it that we had a beautiful home. The two have always been an ideal team. They instilled such wonderful, traditional values in us and gave us a role model for what a marriage and a family should be." She turned to face my parents. "We love you both so much. Thank you for being such amazing parents."

The crowd rose to their feet with their glasses held high to join in the toast. I stood there, stunned. Had we grown up in the same house? How could Brea's picture of our family have been so very different from mine? I wondered what Mary thought, but the way she smiled and nodded in agreement made things perfectly clear.

After the toast, I returned to my table in the corner and found a waiter to refill my glass. I suppose it was only natural, but against the backdrop of my parents' long-lasting marriage, I reflected on the good things about my marriage to Jay. His tireless work ethic, his loyalty to his daughters, and of course, his success as a provider for the family. It made the dismal failure of my divorce seem all the more unreal. Where had things gone so wrong?

When Jay and I separated, I confided in my mother but asked her not to share the news with my father. I wanted to tell him myself when I was ready. I knew he would be angry, and I was afraid of his wrath, even as an adult. However, my mother betrayed my confidence and told him straightaway. From that point on, my parents were coconspirators. Them against me. They regularly called and wrote me letters, demanding that I repent for my sins and return to my husband. They just didn't get it.

My newfound confidence and independent spirit deserted me. Jay had a new wife, and my daughters had gained a stepmom. Where did that leave me? As the party dragged on, I became more and more melancholy. On the one hand, I was happy that my daughters had another woman in their lives—someone who I hoped would nurture them like a caring aunt. On the other hand, I felt a little threatened, unsure of my role as mother and her role as stepmother.

I recalled a song I'd heard in one of the pubs in Ireland. A sad song called "The Town I Love So Well" written by Phil Coulter. A song about growing up in Derry, Northern Ireland, ground zero for The Troubles, and watching the town get torn apart by the warring factions.

For what's done is done and what's won is won
And what's lost is lost and gone forever

When I had heard the song, I experienced a deep feeling of nostalgia. You can't feel nostalgia for a place you've never been before, but substitute "marriage" for "town," and I knew exactly what it was about. There was a place in my heart that would never be the same. It wasn't exactly a hole, more like a scar. I knew it would fade and heal over time, but meanwhile, I needed to move on.

So I did—with a vengeance.

—⁂—

I hit the dating scene like a tornado touching down in a trailer park. I bowled over every man in my path, leaving a scattered trail of courtship victims behind me as I clicked off my castaways. I may have let my standards slip a little in search of a companion, but I didn't have time to find the perfect man. He probably didn't even exist.

Within a few weeks of my immersion into the dating scene, I settled on Dave, a charming man who was sexually adventurous. He sweet-talked me into booking a resort vacation with him. But not just any resort. A Jamaican resort energized by erotic dancing and sensual experiences. It was touted as a place where "everything's included and anything's possible." It offered both a nude beach and a prude beach on the shores of Runaway Bay outside Ocho Rios. The website billed it as "heaven on earth," with its balmy weather, crystal-blue waters, and white sands. I kept the details of my destination under my hat. If my friends and family knew the specifics, they would think I'd gone to Sodom and Gomorrah, a little detour on my way to hell. Grandma Pat, on the other hand, would applaud my exploits.

I was headed for Hedonism—a place known to its enthusiasts as Hedo. It was a resort for swingers, where guests shared more than just their sense of adventure.

Then I got the call that changed everything. I was finalizing my travel plans at my kitchen table when the phone rang.

"I'm leaving your father," my mother said, catching me completely off guard.

"What are you talking about?" I asked as I sank into a chair.

"I'm on my way up to Riverside," she continued. "I'll be there in an hour."

By some odd turn of events, all three of us girls had ended up in Riverside, and my parents had moved from Northern California to Carlsbad in San Diego County to be near their children and grandchildren. Even though our adult family remained geographically close, we were never tight.

"But why?" I asked.

"Because I need to meet with you girls before I discuss anything with your father."

"No, I mean why are you leaving? Did something happen?"

"I'll tell you when I get there," she said and abruptly ended the call. How very like her. Keep the home spotless and take the dirt outside.

I called my new beau, Dave. "We may have to postpone our plans," I said. "Something's come up. My mother needs me."

How strange those words felt coming out of my mouth. But it was true, wasn't it? My mother avoided conflict at all costs. Leaving my father, if she had the guts to go through with it, was going to be extremely difficult for her. I knew how hard it could be.

"Chickening out?" he asked, a taunt in his voice.

"What do you mean?"

"Hedo. You're getting cold feet."

"This has nothing to do with the resort. My mother is leaving my fa—"

"Suuuure."

That's when I realized I didn't want to go to Hedo with Dave. In fact, I didn't want to go *anywhere* with Dave. Effective immediately.

The female delegation of the McNally clan huddled around Brea's dining room table. I nervously stirred my coffee and looked at my mother with questioning eyes as she began to explain.

"Yesterday, I met the children of your father's long-time girlfriend," she announced. Although her hair was perfectly styled, her face looked old and haggard. She had aged since I last saw her at the anniversary party a few months earlier.

"Girlfriend?" I gasped.

"Girlfriend," she confirmed. "A young boy and girl approached me outside of Costco, saying that your father has been messing around with their mother for eight years." The color drained from Mary's face.

"Talk about humiliation," Mom went on. "The boy shouted at me across the parking lot: 'Tell your husband to keep his hands off our mother! She's already got a husband!'"

My mother, a woman who built her life around appearances, lowered her face. Her shoulders started to shake and tears rolled down her cheeks. She must have been absolutely mortified, confronted with her husband's infidelity by a child. She'd been metaphorically wallpapering a house filled with termites for years.

"Does Dad know you know?" I asked.

She extracted a rumpled tissue from inside her sleeve and dabbed at her eyes. "Apparently, the kids told your dad they'd keep quiet if he stopped seeing their mom. He didn't stop, so they found me and told me about the affair. I guess your father didn't care enough to keep it a secret."

"And you believed a pair of kids outside Costco who told you Dad was having an affair?" Mary asked.

"They had proof." My mother withdrew an envelope from her purse and set it down on the table. Hesitantly, I reached for the envelope and pulled out pictures of Dad and a much younger woman in some exotic location.

"My God," I whispered. "She looks like she's my age."

Mom nodded, her lips pursed. "The kids also gave me a pile of love letters and bank statements proving that he's been depositing money into her account for the past eight years," my mother said. "I can't stay. Not after this." Her tears started anew, and I felt my own tears flowing freely down my cheeks.

We sat there, stupefied. No one quite knew what to say. It was all a hoax. A bloody hoax. It had to be.

"I'm so sorry, Mom," I finally said. "I'm so sorry." I got up and went to give my mother a comforting hug. She returned the unexpected embrace in a stilted squeeze, unaccustomed to the open display of affection.

"You can stay here with us," Brea offered.

"Don't be silly," my mother said. "You have your own lives."

We couldn't talk her into staying with any of us, not even for a night. Once she broke the news, she seemed anxious to leave, not wanting consolation or sympathy from her daughters. It was her problem, not ours. She got in her car and drove back to Carlsbad.

I couldn't get over how quickly my parents' marriage had imploded, the hypocrisy of their relationship exposed by a tawdry scene in a Costco parking lot. I tried to make sense of how I'd done the "wrong" thing and broken the rules by getting divorced, while my father had done the "right" thing by keeping a secret from my mother and staying married. His decision didn't seem so right anymore, and mine didn't seem so wrong. At least I'd walked away from my marriage while there was still time for Jay and for me to live full lives. My parents were both in their seventies. I wondered how many days, weeks, months, even years they wished they could have back to do over. In my mind, it was better to take a chance and regret something you did than to regret something you didn't do.

That's when I decided to go to Hedo—alone.

Chapter 13

OPTIONS OPTIONAL

Shortly after my mom dropped the bomb about my dad's affair, I boarded a plane for Jamaica. The demise of my parents' marriage and that of my own left me wondering if traditional relationships were destined for failure. I set out to explore the unconventional. Hedo or bust.

As the plane approached Montego Bay, I sipped a rum and Coke and looked out the window, taking in the legendary landscape. The sunlight fell through lush tropical jungles, spread across the white sand beaches, and spilled into the impossibly blue water. I almost felt as if I could reach out and touch it, and longed to feel its warm rays on body. Whether or not I'd be wearing any clothes when it happened was still very much up in the air.

I was excited by the possibilities: free, wild, and possibly naked. I had never been a "clothing-optional" kind of girl, but maybe I would be in Jamaica. It wasn't as if I had to make up my mind right now. In any case, I was determined not to waste my time. I had missed a lot of sunsets and summer breezes in my life, and I was tired of revisiting the past and worrying about the future. I wanted to live in the now.

My sisters had been anxious about my trip and, I think, more than a little jealous. Younger Mary had whined about how she never got to do anything fun. Older Brea had voiced her matronly disapproval over my irresponsible wanderlust; I think she viewed me as more of a lost soul than a spiritual seeker and told me to stop feeling sorry for myself and seek salvation. Jay had moved on; it was time for me to do the same. In my sisters' eyes, "moving on" meant "settling down." And right up until I left, they called me daily with all kinds of warnings about not drinking the water and steering clear of strange men.

If they only knew.

As soon as I set foot on the tarmac, my body temperature shot up. Fanning myself vigorously with my crinkled boarding pass, I went in search of baggage claim. Fair-skinned tourists and dark-skinned locals milled around me, and as I looked about, it was clear I had ventured someplace faraway. I had difficulty with the island dialect, and I couldn't make out much of what the Jamaicans said. It was like being in Ireland all over again. Only this time, I intended to leave the airport with my luggage.

Once I retrieved my bags, I made my way outside in search of the courtesy shuttle that would take me to the resort. The heat blasted me like a great infernal oven. I stood on the sidewalk, waiting for the bus to appear, willing cool thoughts into my brain. Jamaicans danced and played in the streets as reggae songs blared through loudspeakers. Unlike the regulated rows of taxis at American airports, the Jamaican cabbies solicited fares in a free-form manner. Drivers of all ages gathered around me in a bustling swarm, each man promising a cheaper fare than the next.

As I waited nervously for my shuttle bus, sweat beaded up on my bare skin. I couldn't tell if it was from the humidity or from the morbid picture I was painting in my mind—a shuttle ride in which a naive solo female disappeared into the Jamaican countryside, never to be seen again. Finally, a battered bus with "Hedo" painted in faded white letters on the side pulled up to the curb. I stared at the name on the bus, then pulled out my booking confirmation to double-check the name of the resort. The shabby bus made me doubt my destination and its level of luxury.

The door swung open, and the bus driver—a dark-skinned black man with a wide grin, long dreadlocks, and lean muscular arms—called out, "You going to Hedo, mon?"

"Um ... yes," I said, uncertainly. The bus, the crowds, the humidity—none of it was quite what I had expected.

The driver climbed down from the bus. His name tag read JIMMY. "Well, climb aboard!" he said. He must have sensed my discomfort as he took my luggage to the back of the bus. "No worries, mon. I keep care of you."

Stepping onto the bus, I noted I was the only passenger. While I didn't really expect the driver to be naked, I was relieved to see that he was fully clothed.

The bus was musty and hot, and a spring from the seat dug into my thigh. I shifted over slightly and just missed getting skewered by another wayward spring. I switched seats as the driver bounded back onto the bus and cranked it into gear. We lurched forward and made our slow departure from the airport, on the wrong side of the road again.

"You traveling alone, mon?" the driver called back to me.

"Yes. My ex-husband just remarried, so I'm treating myself to my own honeymoon." I don't know why I spilled my guts like that. I guess my sisters' words about feeling sorry for myself stung after all. I was determined not to play the victim. I was the author of my own adventure.

"You got the right idea, mon. It's a savage country. Anything goes."

"I didn't know you drive on the wrong—I mean opposite—side of the road here." Overgrown trees rustled against my open window as we rushed down the road.

"We used to be ruled by England. That's why we drive on the side opposite you Americans. In 1962, we gained our independence." His dark eyes flashed, as he shot a quick glance at me in his rearview mirror.

"So, what's the resort like?"

He let out a hearty howl and looked into his mirror again. "Oh, you got the right place for a honeymoon. They like to swing from the vines over there!"

Swinging. Was it really that out in the open? The only swinging I'd ever done had been on swing sets when I was a kid. I leaned forward a bit.

"Do people really walk around naked all day?" I asked, resting my elbow on the seat ahead of me.

"Oh, no, mon. Not everyone, anyway. Clothing *optional*," he said.

Jimmy told me he was originally from Kingston and was married with five kids. He'd never been to the States, and he was full of questions about my homeland. From his inquiries, I could tell he was trying to conceptualize such a vast and diverse country. Was it true that it snowed in the mountains? Had I been to the Statue of Liberty? How long did it take to get from one coast to the other? Were there any jobs for drivers? Were the people friendly?

He wanted to come to the States but couldn't without a sponsor. When I realized that he couldn't leave the island, it dawned on me that—much to my dismay—I took my freedom for granted. My thoughts turned to how I had made excuses to stay in my marriage, how I hadn't traveled when I was a self-imprisoned wife. Like Jimmy, I had been trapped in what others probably thought was paradise.

Jimmy and I talked for a while longer and then rode in silence for several miles. I gazed out the open window and saw a church at nearly every intersection. My father's grandfather had been a missionary in Jamaica. He left my great-grandmother in Idaho with nine children while he went to the Caribbean to reform "the heathens" in the name of God.

"Why are there so many missionaries in Jamaica?" I wondered aloud, curious to hear his thoughts.

Jimmy's lyrical laughter echoed through the empty bus. "If you were a missionary, where would you want to go?"

He had a point. When I was young, I had participated in medical missions to Mexico and the Canary Islands through my church. The towns were poor, but the setting was always tropical and exotic. I never wondered about it then, but it seemed to fit what Jimmy was saying. It got awfully cold in Idaho during the winter.

"There are more churches per square mile here than anywhere else in the world. It's a business. The preachers have the nicest cars and biggest houses."

The town outside my window confirmed what he was saying. "Do Jamaicans feel like they've been helped by all the missionaries?"

"Ha! The missionaries tell everybody to accept their suffering and to look forward to happiness in the next life. This is not the Rasta way. Rastas believe in pleasure now, mon." Jimmy reached up and adjusted his rearview mirror, which had tilted sideways on the bumpy road.

"I thought all Jamaicans were Rastafarians."

"Not all. Rastafari is a religion like any other. Our God is Jah. We are free of mental slavery. We live life with a true heart and one love."

"I like that," I said, once again setting my boarding pass to work as a fan.

Jimmy continued, telling me that Rastafarians were a peaceful and loving people who didn't support anybody who would go to war, fight, or kill. And much of their lifestyle revolved around reggae, which was more than just music. It was about the attainment of freedom and emancipation through peaceful means. Rastafarians believed heaven was right here on Earth, not somewhere else. Since they believed their body was a temple, they didn't need brick-and-mortar churches. So maybe Jimmy didn't feel as trapped in paradise as I had assumed.

I was surprised when he told me that he knew the Bible backward and forward because that's how he learned to read. He didn't attend church; he believed God was within him.

"Dreads are our antennas for reaching Jah." Jimmy gestured to me. "You got long hair. So you got a good connection. Irie!"

I laughed. It seemed to me that the Rastafarians had done the same as the Celtic Christians—taken bits and pieces from other religions and made them their own. The world over, I was finding an amalgamation of different religions, all seeking the same thing. My time in Ireland had opened me up to new viewpoints regarding organized religion, made me less judgmental. My curiosity was growing, and I found out the more I learned, the more I didn't know. Seeing the world though other people's eyes proved exciting. I was slowly losing my biases—or at least I liked to think I was.

"So, you like Bob Marley?" Jimmy asked.

"Sure," I said. "I don't know many of his songs, though."

Jimmy laughed that hearty laugh again. "I'm not talking about the singer, mon."

I caught Jimmy's eyes in the rearview mirror as it hit me that Bob Marley was code for ganja. Weed, pot, wacky tobaccy.

"Oh, *that* Bob Marley," I replied. "I can't say I'm all that familiar with it." The bus hit a large pothole, and I bounced up off my seat.

"Well, if you want to start your honeymoon on the right foot ..."

Jimmy reached underneath his seat and pulled out a plastic bag filled with weed. He shook it at me, never taking his eyes off the road.

"What you say? Forty dollars, US."

I looked at the baggie. I'd never smoked so much as a cigarette, and now I was being offered a whole bag of marijuana. I turned and looked out the rear window to make sure we weren't being watched. We had left Montego Bay behind, and the road stretched out, a narrow track in the tropical jungle, deserted in both directions.

"I don't know," I said. "I don't even know how to roll a joint. And isn't it illegal?"

"I take care of everything. Ganja may not be legal here, but the authorities have more important laws to enforce. This one, they let slide. No worries, mon."

Jimmy eased the bus over to a wide spot on the shoulder and

engaged the parking brake. He pulled some rolling papers out of his pocket and shut off the engine. He sat down in the seat across from me. Not a car or person in sight. I looked out the window and saw nothing but dense jungle, thick with palms, ferns, and bushy masses of flowering plants.

"Now," Jimmy said as he opened the bag, releasing a pungent aroma. "If you want maximum impact from the irie incense, you got to spread it evenly and roll it tight." His fingers moved expertly as he extracted some weed from the bag, sprinkled it inside the paper, and sealed it, all in the blink of an eye. He held it up for my inspection.

"Nice," I said, as if I knew the difference between good joint and a bad one.

Jimmy quickly rolled a few more. When he was finished, he lit one of the smaller ones and took a big hit. Then he handed it to me. I stared at the smoking joint, unsure what to do next. I'd never had my Bill Clinton "experimental" moment in college. Jay didn't approve. Well, screw him.

I brought the joint to my lips, took a tentative puff, and quickly blew out the smoke. "I don't feel anything," I said.

"You got to inhale deeper, mon. Get the full effect."

He motioned for me to try again. I squared my shoulders, inhaled deeply, and collapsed in a coughing fit.

"Slower, mon." Jimmy laughed as he took the joint away from me. "Slower."

"I don't think I'm cut out for this," I said as I struggled to catch my breath. My throat burned, and my lungs felt mildly polluted.

Jimmy puffed away as if he were breathing clean mountain air. "You'll get the hang of it. Irie!"

"Okay," I whispered and took another drag, hoping to fully experience the moment and enjoy life to the very core. I held the smoke in my lungs for the briefest of moments before blowing it out in a slow, steady stream.

Jimmy smiled. "You see, mon? No worries, huh?"

I nodded, getting the hang of it. "None at all," I said. I leaned back against the seat and floated up to the ceiling, where everything was more intense. The dull colors of the bus turned vibrant, and the silence rang loudly in my ears. I could smell Jimmy's sweat and my own perspiration. We sat in silence, puffing away, and my mind swirled in a kaleidoscope of images from church services and Communion sacraments gone by.

"How long have you smoked weed?" I asked when I came back down to earth.

Jimmy shrugged. "Long as I can remember." He took another puff and pointed at himself. "Rasta, mon. That's what we do."

I took another drag. My arms and legs felt like jelly. My family would die, absolutely die, if they could see me.

"We smoke ganja because we believe we are to burn incense in the temple of Jah, and our body is our temple. Ganja opens us up so we can better relate to Jah."

"I think I'm having a religious experience right now," I said as I took another hit.

I felt a laugh bubble from my lips. At least I thought it was my lips. I put a hand over my mouth to suppress the giggles, but laughter burst through my fingers anyway. I doubled over in hysterics and held my head in my hands, thinking of all the times I'd eaten the body and drunk the blood of Christ during Sunday Communion at my Baptist church. Tears started to stream down my face, I was laughing so hard. "God is here!" I said, pointing to myself.

Jimmy smiled and took one last drag from his joint. "You a Rasta now, mon."

In Ireland, I had discovered things I didn't know about myself. I had vowed to allow myself more pleasure and to explore higher peaks. My experience on the Jamaican bus was not exactly what I had envisioned when I made that promise, but I couldn't deny it—I was filled with pleasure and higher than a kite.

Jimmy stood. "Time to go," he said as he got back behind the wheel.

"Are you okay to drive?"

He laughed. "It takes more than half a joint to lay me out."

It was more than half, I thought. I'd only had a few puffs. Jimmy had taken up my slack and smoked most of the joint himself. I settled back in my seat to enjoy the rest of the journey. We motored through tropical groves and occasionally passed brightly painted houses. Everything seemed so vivid. It began to rain, and I felt the droplets splash against my face through the open window. I closed my eyes and let the hot breeze and cool rain wash over me. I took a huge gulp of fresh air, relishing the scent of the rain and easing the slight burn I still felt in the back of my throat. I opened my eyes, amazed to see how radiant and colorful the world looked. The rain had turned Jamaica even more fresh and fragrant. Or maybe the pot was responsible for the transformation.

Jimmy pulled into a circular driveway in front of the resort. Huge palm trees framed a regal salmon-colored building, and hibiscus and agapanthus bloomed around the entry. "Welcome to Hedo, mon."

I leaned forward, steadying myself on the seat. "I think you already welcomed me."

"What did I tell you? Good way to start a honeymoon."

"No kidding."

I pulled out two twenties and gave them to Jimmy. He slipped me the ganja. I peered into the baggie and was glad to see the extra joints he had rolled on the bus. That would save me the trouble of having to master the technique right away. As I stashed the ganja in my purse, Jimmy ran to retrieve my luggage. When he returned, his smile was gone and he addressed me solemnly.

"Don't be afraid to embrace your divinity, and don't be less than you are. Celebrate the sacred. Don't waste time being small."

I didn't know what to say. Was that the "full effect" Jimmy had promised, or part of Rastafarian indoctrination? Was I taking him a bit too seriously or not seriously enough?

He winked at me as he handed me my suitcase. "Enjoy your stay, mon, and have a beautiful day."

As Jimmy drove off, I took in my surroundings. Low buildings with a simple, island feel stretched along the length of the resort. People milled about in bare feet and swimsuits, some with drinks in hand. Laughter danced across the grounds as reggae music blared. Hedo.

I headed toward the entrance where I must have registered. Certainly, someone handed me a key and led me to my room. I didn't remember any of it. I just floated along, waiting for a naked person to appear every time I turned a corner. But I didn't see a single one. There were no orgies in full swing; everything looked perfectly normal. I didn't know if I was disappointed or relieved. The ganja had left me feeling a bit outside of myself.

Once in my room, I sighed and collapsed into a large chair. I couldn't tell if I was exhausted from my travels or simply stoned. The room was clean and airy, with oversize windows and a tropical pink-and-yellow bedspread that vibrated with energy. A ceiling-mounted mirror was strategically positioned above the bed. I moved from the chair to the bed, where I stretched out on my back and giggled at the smiling woman I saw looking down at me.

The ocean lay just steps from my patio, and I decided to take a swim. I fished my bathing suit out of my bag. Normally, I'd unpack all of my clothes and neatly arrange them in drawers, but that could wait. I wanted to play in the Caribbean Sea. I slid open my patio door and was about to walk out when I remembered the ganja. I didn't want to leave my newly purchased contraband in my purse. I opened the bureau drawer to stash my weed next to the ubiquitous copy of Gideon's Bible. A perfect, albeit sacrilegious, hiding place.

But there was no Bible. Instead, I found … more pot. A baggie similar to my own bulged in the corner of the drawer. Was that the Jamaican version of chocolate mints on the pillows? Did all the guests receive such hospitality, or had the room's previous occupants hidden their stash in the same place that I'd thought to hide mine? I tucked my weed alongside the other bag and headed out the patio door.

I scanned the beach. No naked people there either, just a couple sprawled next to each other on striped beach towels. I walked through a bougainvillea-lined pathway toward the surf, dropped my towel in the sand, and waded into the clear blue water. I felt the pull of the tide around my ankles, then my legs, then my whole body. I was still under the influence of the pot, and the ebb-and-flow sensation of the sea was exhilarating. I took a deep breath of the salty air and scrunched my toes into the wet sand. I let the gentle waves carry me along until I was floating. It seemed incomprehensible that I was really there, that any of it was true. It looked like paradise, smelled like paradise, and felt like paradise. Was it?

—⁂—

Like in Ireland, I was afraid to leave my room that first night and face the other vacationers. I wanted to blame the ganja for making me self-conscious to the point of paranoia, but since the same thing happened at Mrs. McNally's B&B, I knew it wasn't just the marijuana. I was starving, however, and that I definitely could blame on the weed. Since there was no such thing as room service at Hedo, I couldn't hide in my quarters and eat by myself. I debated about taking a quick hit from my hidden treasure, just in case people really were swinging from vines as Jimmy suggested. My ex-boyfriend Dave had encouraged me to consider swinging along with the other guests, but the thought frightened me, especially since I was at Hedo alone. Even though I'd had a passionate encounter with a complete stranger in Ireland and had just smoked pot with a dreadlocked bus driver, I wasn't ready to call myself a swinging single.

As I walked to the outdoor dining room, I took a few deep breaths. I was nervous about what I might see. At first, the dining area seemed like any other hotel buffet, with serving tables that stretched from one end of the room to the other. When I looked again, I placed my hand over my heart to still the pounding. Gathered about the dining tables, men and women sat stark naked, nonchalantly eating their meals while chatting with others. I had to fight the urge to giggle and flee the room. I was sure I'd never be brave enough to "go native," but for a moment, I felt out of place simply because I was clothed.

When I looked around the room a little longer, trying not to stare, I noticed that not everyone was nude. Some were dressed in casual beachwear. The kitchen staff were dressed in crisp uniforms. They carefully tended the buffet to ensure that the mounds of food were always piled high. I had a serious case of the munchies, so I focused on the food—steaming platters of fish and chicken, beef and pork, rice dishes with julienned vegetables, and wedges of fresh fruit.

Still in a bit of a stupor, I grabbed a plate from the buffet table and marveled at the spread, tempted by oysters and martinis, sushi and sake, desserts and Champagne, and of course, traditional Jamaican cuisine and rum. There was as much alcohol as there was food, and I was ready to indulge in it all. I loaded up on island specialties, neatly labeled for the uninitiated—jerk chicken, rice and peas, curry goat, and even a small cup of oxtail soup.

Balancing my plate in one hand and a Mai Tai in the other, I found a seat at a table with a young man and woman, an older couple, and a pair of girls who I guessed to be in their twenties. Only the older couple was nude. As a physical therapist, I'd seen many naked bodies, but in a social setting, the nudity struck me as comical. Still, I admired the lack of pretense, especially in the older couple whose bodies sagged with age and wrinkles. The raging appetite that had driven me to the dining room deserted me, but I set my plate down anyway. I could at least sit across from naked people and carry on a casual conversation, couldn't I?

"Hi, I'm Barbara," I said, wishing I had a partner for protection and security. Even Dave would have been a welcome companion at that moment.

A round of "hellos" went up from the table. We exchanged the usual pleasantries, and I wondered who the swingers in the group were. I learned that the young couple was honeymooning, the girls were French, and the older hedonists were in their seventies. I had a hard time listening to the older couple. Whenever I looked at them, my concentration—which already suffered from the pot—lapsed into visions of septuagenarian sex that I wished I could banish from my brain. I found myself scrutinizing everything my fellow diners said. Were these people really interested in my sparkling conversation, or were they sizing me up so they could make me their love slave?

After a few refills of my Mai Tai, I felt my inhibitions begin to slip away. "So, what brings you two to Jamaica?" I asked the two French girls, one brunette and one blonde. They seemed shy, and I figured they were the "safest."

"We come to Jamaica one week every year to be naked on the beach, swim in the warm water, and find a ménage à trois," the brunette said.

I almost spit out my drink. I'd never heard someone talk about a threesome so casually.

"Really?" I asked, wide-eyed. "Like, with a guy and … each other?" I eyed their svelte figures and concluded that they wouldn't have any trouble finding a willing man.

They both laughed. "But of course!" said the blonde one. "We like to, how you say, play all day and all night. Sex, it is so much fun. Ménage à trois and being naked, it is no different than … trying a new restaurant."

I gulped my drink and shook my head. "I don't think I could do it. Swinging or the other thing."

"You may love it," the brunette teased, "and find that you want to return every year like we do!"

The gray-haired old man leaned back in his chair and folded arthritic fingers over his potbelly. "They're right," he said. "Don't knock it until you try it. We've been coming here for over twenty years."

"It's made our marriage stronger," his wife said, snuggling closer to him.

I couldn't imagine having a swinging marriage. Of course, I was the one who was divorced, and they were still together, so what did I know?

I finished off my Mai Tai and stumbled back to my room—alone. I couldn't fall asleep right away. My mind swirled with naked bodies and fat doobies. Nearly all the people I met that night were urban professionals who used their annual visit to Hedo to escape their usual routines and buttoned-down lives. They made it sound so sane.

I thought of Grandma Pat and her boudoir pictures. She would have felt right at home at Hedo. I was pretty sure my grandparents weren't swingers, but I recalled seeing *Playboy* magazines at their home, so I knew they were curious and open about their sexuality. I was open to learning more about the lifestyle, but that was about as far as I could go. I just couldn't see myself participating in a threesome or eating dinner naked.

Maybe, I told myself, I just preferred a little bit of intimacy with my sex. Still, there was something liberating and exhilarating about the thought of running around naked and engaging in sex just for fun. The resort was filled with people who didn't feel self-conscious about their bodies and who were candid about their sexual relations. I had a body I was proud of and a playful attitude about sex. So why couldn't I be one of them?

Chapter 14

CONSERVATIVE HEDONISM

When it came to the clothing-optional beach, I stuck with the clothing option. I figured that once I got to the beach and made myself comfortable in my one-piece bathing suit, I could drop my defenses and strip away my pretenses. Or try to anyway. Baby steps, Barbara, baby steps.

Beneath a cloudless sky, the waves smoothed the narrow stretch of white sand, rhythmically hiding it underwater, then exposing it to the sun. The private beach was small and secluded, but it was crowded with guests from the resort. I searched for a place away from the continuous parade of nudity. Naked bodies of all shapes, sizes, hues, and ages wandered the beach—some taut and fit, others rippling with excess rolls. I watched a man walk by, his member dangling freely, flopping from side to side as he strolled in the sand. It looked uncomfortable to me, but what did I know? The women exposed an assortment of bare breasts, from well-proportioned and perky to sagging and tired. I did spot a few other conservative souls in swimwear, but we were the exceptions.

I put down my towel, slathered on sunscreen, and began my day's work of soaking up as much sun as possible. A clad flower amongst a field of nudes, I lay down and closed my eyes. I took a few deep breaths and felt my apprehension slip away. Soon, the chatter of the beach lulled me to sleep, and I dreamed I was among the naked bodies frolicking in the surf.

"Is this spot taken?"

The man's voice jolted me awake. A gorgeous couple towered over me, scantily attired, but thankfully, not nude. He wore a green, yellow, and black Speedo (the colors of the Jamaican flag), and she a white thong bikini. My first thought was that a pair of swingers had targeted me for their fun and games. I couldn't help but stare at his obviously large package and her voluptuous breasts, barely covered by two small triangles of Spandex.

"Excuse me?" I said, instinctively reaching for my T-shirt, a throwback response to my childhood when modest girls covered up around others.

The man gestured to the spot beside me. "May we join you? I'm afraid there aren't many free spots left on the beach."

I looked about. The beach was overrun with nude bodies. "Um, sure. Go ahead."

"Thank you, thank you," he said as the two of them laid out their towels next to mine.

The woman—a tall, striking blonde with dark skin and a tiny waist—held out her hand to me. "I'm Renata. This is my husband, Paulo."

"I'm Barbara," I said, squinting against the sun.

She lay down on the towel next to mine and stretched out her long legs. "We're from Brazil—Rio. Have you been?"

"Never, but I love your accent. Portuguese, right?"

"Yes. We come to Jamaica every year," Paulo said. "It's our home away from home." Like Renata, he was tall and dark, with smooth, defined muscles.

"Barbara, I have to tell you that, in our language, we don't really make the distinction between acquaintance and friend. We use the word *amigo*," Renata said. "We are all amigos here, yes?" She spilled coconut-scented oil over her perfect body, then rubbed it in, putting on a sensual show for the casual onlooker. When she had finished, she passed the oil to Paulo.

Here it comes, I thought. Less than an hour on the beach and I was already being invited to an orgy by a couple of oiled-up Brazilians. I tried to set aside my suspicions. "Yes," I ventured. "We are all amigos."

They didn't try to seduce me. We just talked. Renata was a corporate attorney, and Paulo a professional photographer. They'd been married for ten years and had no kids, preferring to spend their time and money on the pursuit of travel and new experiences.

Renata propped herself up on her elbow and tilted her head toward me. "Barbara, I do not understand how you can wear so much clothing. Aren't you hot?" she asked.

I still wore the T-shirt I had put on when they had approached. "Well, in America, our beaches are a little more conservative, so that's what I'm used to. I suspect the beaches in Brazil are more like the beaches here." I felt the grit of the sand on my cheek as I tucked my hair behind my ear.

Paulo sat cross-legged on his towel, surveying the beach. "Yes, yes, it is very much like home, though you see way more thongs in Brazil."

"In Portuguese, we call a thong *fio de dental*—dental floss," Renata explained.

"But just because a woman wears a thong doesn't mean she is loose," Paulo added. "We are very uninhibited and proud of our bodies." They definitely had bodies to be proud of.

"Well, I can't speak for all of America," I said, "but I can tell you about my own upbringing. Every year, I went to church camp, where we were required to wear T-shirts over our swimsuits to show our modesty."

Renata gasped. "That's the most ridiculous thing I've ever heard." She shook her head. "Why, all this cover-up-the-body? It's c-r-r-razy," she said, rolling her *r*'s.

"I think the camp counselors were trying to scare us. They told us that if we were immodest, we might tempt the young boys to want to have sex with us, which was considered a sin. We were also forbidden to dance, wear makeup, or paint our fingernails."

"What a terrible way to grow up," Renata said.

"Oh, it could have been worse." I shrugged and remembered how some of the evangelical kids at camp were miniature versions of my father, full of fire and brimstone and eager to preach. But isn't that what Renata and Paulo were doing? Preaching the benefits of living life without inhibitions?

I didn't want to defend my country or my upbringing to my new amigos. I went to Hedo to have fun, not to be converted to a lifestyle that didn't suit me or defend a way of living that was no longer appealing to me. As the couple walked toward the water, I peeled off my T-shirt, stretched out, and reclined on the sand. Lying on that Jamaican beach with frothy waves splashing against the shore, I drifted off to sleep again. Perhaps I'd get naked some other time.

—※—

Some other time proved to be that same day—late in the afternoon.

Although the beach was clothing optional, the resort's swimming pools were segregated into two groups: nude and prude. While both pools had a swim-up bar, there was hardly anyone in the prude pool. The nude pool had more vitality, so I picked it. It's what Grandma Pat would have done—because of the people, not the nudity. I stripped off my bathing suit and dove in.

Underwater, all I could hear was my own frenetic heartbeat; the music and laughter died away. Why was I so nervous? Wasn't this what I came for? When I resurfaced, I felt as if I'd been dropped into a European film scene. People ate poolside aphrodisiacs and drank the free-flowing cocktails. I swam to the bar, ordered a rum and Coke, and soon found myself staring into a cup filled with nothing but ice.

Although the sun had begun its daily retreat, the water still felt warm on my naked body, whetting my appetite for another cocktail, faintly stirring my libido. It wasn't so bad. In fact, it felt pretty great. As I waited my turn at the swim-up bar, the man next to me ordered a front-end lifter, a drink made with ginger wine and Red Bull.

"Honey, don't you think he's hot?" he asked.

At first I thought he was talking to me, but a petite woman on the other side of him leaned in for a closer inspection before she answered. "Oh, definitely," she said. "He's very handsome."

"If you want to use him as a toy, go ahead. We'll both pleasure you," the man said to her, winking at me. I glanced at the ring on his finger, then at the one on hers. They seemed to be a couple. The alcohol had loosened my inhibitions, so I fired off a question.

"Don't you get jealous?" I asked the man.

"Oh, I don't own her," he answered. "She's my wife, not my possession."

"Yeah, but ..." I looked past him at his attractive spouse. Her wet hair was slicked back in a way that accentuated her high cheekbones and her almond-shaped eyes. "Isn't that a dangerous proposition, even if you approve?"

"What bonds us together is love and respect, not sexual exclusivity."

"We have our boundaries," his wife said. "We only share when the other person is present, and we won't kiss someone else."

The woman leaned over and squeezed her husband's arm. He looked at her affectionately. Although their words sounded rehearsed, like a speech they'd given many times before, they were clearly in love with each other.

We were several minutes into our conversation when I realized I was talking to complete strangers about extramarital sex while sitting at a nude swim-up bar where the water only came up to my waist. My breasts were fully exposed. Was it the conversation with the two of them that helped me let go of my inhibitions or was it the alcohol?

"Every couple here defines their own rules," the man said. "For us, an affair of the heart crosses the line between sexual intimacy and emotional intimacy. The emotional affairs are the dangerous ones."

He spoke from behind a pair of mirrored sunglasses, so I had no idea where he was looking. I surreptitiously crossed my arms over my breasts in a way that I hoped looked casual, not conservative.

"It's unrealistic to think that married people aren't going to feel the occasional desire for someone new," he went on. "We're no different. We're just honest—with ourselves and with each other."

He looked like an ordinary guy, once I got past the fact that he was naked. With his generous midsection and his short, bristled hair, he resembled a well-fed porcupine. He could have easily been one of Jay's buddies, but our discussion was a far cry from the standard Riverside dinner-party conversations about stock markets and home prices. And I was a long way from the guarded exchanges that had comprised conversations in my parents' house.

People at Hedo weren't trying to keep up appearances. They were letting themselves go. I wondered how it might have changed my marriage if Jay and I had been that open. We might have realized that sex (or the lack of it) was not as important as love, respect, honesty, sharing, and acceptance of the other as a person, not a possession. Those were the building blocks of a successful marriage.

"If someone else can bring pleasure to my wife," he said, "I'm happy to share her. As adults, we can define our marriage any way we want."

"We share any toy we bring into our bed," she continued. "There are no secrets."

A relationship without secrets. That was a novel idea and a rare find, but at least these people were open about sex. Contemplating the level of self-confidence that this demanded, I wondered how they learned to be so open about their eroticism. I tried to imagine sharing a lover with Jay. No way, José. John Wayne didn't swing. But did I?

I turned on my submerged bar stool and looked across the pool.

Lounge chairs neatly ringed the edge of the water. The lights winked on, and their reflection shimmered on the surface. Most of the swimmers had given up their exercise in favor of a drink, and those still in the water clustered around the swim-up bar. Naked, of course.

"So, what brings you here?" the wife asked.

"I needed a vacation," I answered. I realized how lame that sounded—and dishonest. "I recently got a divorce, and when I heard my ex got remarried, I decided it was time for me to have some fun."

"Good for you," the woman said. "You're showing your true spirit just by being here. You should come to the toga party tonight. It will be great fun!"

"I might just do that."

I swam to the other side of the pool and collected my bathing suit. Wrapped in a towel, I headed back to my room. I began to think that, as much as the people at Hedo seemed to have their lives under control, the swinger's lifestyle couldn't be as carefree as I had been imagining. There were all those relationships to negotiate. Swingers probably ran the same risks other married couples did, maybe even more. But they seemed to live their lives so fully that their unfulfilled desires—if they had any—didn't spill forth in deceitful ways. Perhaps one result of this honest approach was that both partners felt accepted for who they really were.

—⁂—

I hadn't packed a toga in my suitcase, so I squeezed into the next best thing—a tiny white tank top and a white stretch miniskirt. Dressed in an outfit more age-appropriate for my daughters, I slipped on my sandals and left for the party.

Outside my door, I picked a few blue hibiscus blossoms and slipped them behind my ear. The walkways were heady with tropical fragrance. Fuchsia flames of bougainvillea spilled over the low walls, and the wind rustled through the palm trees. Crickets sang to me, and a lizard scampered across my path. I shivered, feeling the twilight's electricity.

I stepped onto the sand and snatched up my sandals. The contagious beat of steel drums pulsed through the air, and I could hear laughing and the clinking of glasses as I walked toward the music. Island energy ran hot, and that evening's party, Caesar's Taboo, promised to be a scorcher. To make both nudes and prudes feel welcome, the party was billed as "Costume (or Clothing) Required." Things were likely to loosen up later in the week, but this party was an icebreaker.

Hammocks hung between the palms, bodies pressed against the woven ropes, and I heard two women giggling as I passed. The nightclub was just ahead. It was covered by a thatched roof, but open on the sides.

"A Red Stripe, please," I said as I found a place at the bar inside the club. A few minutes later, two tall black women sat down next to me.

"That's kinda bitter," said the woman closest to me, eyeing my beer before she ordered her own and one for her friend.

"You may need some white rum to wash it down," said the other.

They both wore tall heels and dresses that were every bit as tight as my skirt. I looked jealously at their smooth, unwrinkled faces and wondered if skin like that was part of the magic of island humidity. Neither wore much makeup, but they were natural beauties, with eyes so dark they were almost black, and figures that did justice to the dresses they wore.

"Honey, I'm Irish and Guinness runs through my veins, so bring it on!" I said. I held up my beer, and the women picked up theirs. The three of us clinked bottles.

"Cheers," I said.

"Irie," they replied in unison.

The woman to my left took a long draw of her beer. "Ah," she said. "Like a cold, smooth ribbon. My name is Alisha. You?"

"Barbara." I offered my hand. Alisha ignored it and leaned over to give me a friendly Jamaican squeeze.

"Laticia," said her friend, and we nodded.

The club was just beginning to fill up, as guests filtered in wearing togas that varied in length and design. Most outfits looked like a loosely draped bed sheet, held together by a rope tied around the waist. One woman even wore a crown of leaves on her head.

"You live on the island?" I asked, guessing from their accents.

"Yeah. We having a girls' night tonight," Laticia answered. "We bought a Naughty Night Pass so we could come to the toga party."

I drank more Red Stripe, and some of it dribbled down my chin. The cold liquid trailed across my hot skin.

"Oh, this is my jam!" Laticia popped out of her chair and began to gyrate slowly on the rough-planked dance floor. Once she started to dance, others began to join in. They got up from hammocks and bar seats and began to sway, togas fluttering in the breeze. Alisha joined Laticia and began to grind her hips against her friend, closing her eyes and mouthing the lyrics. I found my way to the dance floor, too. The music filled my body, speeding up, then slowing down, and finally settling into a steady beat. I held my bottle by its short neck and moved to the pulse of the music.

Alisha didn't approve of my moves. "We need to loosen you up some more," she said as she signaled the bartender for another round. "Show you how we do it in Jamaica."

Laticia collected the fresh beers and distributed one to each of us. "Irie!" we shouted, joining bottles in another toast.

Several men with open shirts joined the dance. I started to feel giddy, and my hips and arms began to unspool. The crowd let out a cheer when the DJ introduced a favorite song.

"You have to do it like this," Alisha said as she rocked her hips in a nasty circle and started to chant along with the song. She took my hands in hers and turned me around in a slow, gentle motion.

"See," Laticia said, imitating Alisha's movements. "Roll your hips like this. Nice and easy. Pretend like you're having sex."

I rotated the lower half of my body like a belly dancer, mimicking the moves they showed me. Buoyed by the beer, I ran my free hand up and down my body, relishing the sheer joy of its movement. I swirled my arms in the air, then swiveled my body, as if I were an exotic pole dancer. Laticia came up behind me while Alisha stood in front, and we ground around our little spot like a trio of sexy swingers. I let down my hair and shook it free, shimmying even more. Laticia put her hands on my shoulders, and we began to sway together. I let my body shift into new positions, savoring the sensations. The music played on, and what was left of my inhibitions slid out of me into the puddle of spilled beer beneath my feet.

Sweaty bodies bumped in a free-form rhythm, and the crowded space pumped with an erotic energy. I lost sight of Alisha and Laticia, then felt a pair of muscular hands grip my waist from behind. I gasped, but before I could turn around, a sandpapery patch of skin nuzzled my neck. Warm breath flooded my ear.

"Me like the way you move, miss," the mysterious stranger said as he slowed my body down to match the wavelike motion of his.

I spotted Alisha and Laticia near the bar. They both shrugged and gave me a thumbs-up. I turned around to find myself staring at tufts of black chest hair and ropes of gold chains. Looking up, I saw a face shadowed with a day-old beard. The man had full lips and perfect teeth, and I pegged him to be in his midtwenties.

"Toby," he said.

Without a word, we began to move together, eyes locked, hypnotized by the music. Toby pressed one broad hand against the small of my back and clasped my hand with his other, then dipped me toward the floor. He brought me back up and twirled me face forward, then he encircled me from behind with his lean arms.

When the song ended, I stepped back from Toby. He looked at me with steely eyes and flashed a brilliant smile. His raw male energy exuded a complex scent of beer, sweat, and cologne. He was bold, forward, and too much to handle. Dancing with Toby was nothing like the sweet, heady embrace of Alisha and Laticia. I thanked him for the dance and blew him a kiss as I went in search of my new friends. He waved and turned his attention to a girl in a pink bikini top and cut-off shorts.

The music seemed to get louder and the space more crowded as the alcohol went to my head. I danced until I thought I'd melt from the heat of the bopping bodies. I broke through the crowd to take a breather outside, where a cool breeze skimmed over me. I steadied myself against a palm tree.

A hand rested lightly on my hip, and I turned to see Alisha's smiling face. Her lips shone with a rosy gloss, and everything about her looked soft.

"Drunk, honey?" she whispered.

"Just resting up for the next song." In truth, I was a little woozy.

Alisha raised her eyebrows, gesturing toward a hammock suspended from the tree. "I came looking for you," she said.

"I'm just here for the party."

Alisha smiled and leaned forward, her lips coming to meet mine. I opened my mouth to … protest? Maybe. But only for a second. I parted my lips, and they met hers. We kissed. She tasted like sweet honey and salt water. I wanted to be closer to Alisha—not necessarily in a sexual way, but in a sensual feminine bond that I hadn't anticipated.

"You ready to dance now," she said.

She took my hand and pulled me to the dance floor. We danced for hours, and before I knew it, fluorescent lights signaled the end of the party. I was drenched in sweat and had bound my hair onto the top of my head in a primitive knot. Alisha and Laticia looked drained, too. The faint remnants of red lipstick still rimmed their lips, and they each held a pair of mammoth high heels in their hands. The first purple strains of dawn were overtaking the night.

Together, we walked barefoot back toward my room. My body ached with equal parts excitement and exhaustion. As we rounded the corner near my door, Alisha held my hand, kissed me softly on the cheek, and whispered in my ear, "Come swim in the nude pool with us, honey."

I wasn't drunk anymore, but I could barely keep my eyes open. If I got into a pool, I'd surely sink to the bottom. "After I get some rest," I mumbled.

Alisha took my face in her hands and put her lips on mine. Her mouth opened, and I felt mine do the same. I closed my eyes and relaxed into the tingling sensation of her probing tongue and her smooth Jamaican curves. So much gentler than a man.

"You get some sleep," she whispered as she left. "There's a lot more excitement on the horizon."

I hoped she was right. Inside my head, the steel drums pounded out their rhythms such that I didn't know where my body ended and the music began or where my desires started and fantasies took over. I tumbled into bed and immediately fell into a deep sleep and dreamed about Wiccans and women and the magic of both.

Chapter 15

FLOATING IN FEAR

The nude pool was packed with people, and for once they weren't naked. Instead of sporting bloated bellies and sagging breasts, they were encased in neoprene. Was that another fetish I didn't know about? It turned out to be a scuba lesson—the only clothing-*not*-optional event at the resort.

I watched from beneath a wide hat as I lounged poolside on a puffy chaise. Soon, the instructor, his hair bleached blond by the sea and the sun, shuffled over in his flip-flops and asked if I was interested in scuba. I told him I was, and just like that, he signed me up for a beginner's class.

The next afternoon, I donned a wetsuit, slung an oxygen tank over my shoulder, and tightened the straps to secure the tank to my back. I pulled a mask over my face and left the regulators hanging free as I wriggled into a pair of fins. How I was supposed to swim with all that stuff on?

I descended the stairs into the pool, my finned feet the size of a giant's. When I pushed off into the water, I floated back to the surface. Amazing!

During the class, the instructor, Tim, taught us how to breathe oxygen from the tank and how to use the gauges to measure oxygen levels. He showed us how to establish buoyancy by using a device called a buoyancy compensator. After a short break, he instructed us on how to remove and replace our masks underwater and how to retrieve our regulators. He also demonstrated the emergency technique of buddy breathing, in which one diver breathes oxygen from another diver's tank.

"Scuba diving is much more exciting than snorkeling," Tim said. "Snorkeling is like watching porn, and scuba diving is like being the star."

Sex seemed to be on the menu 24/7 at Hedo. I wanted to become a certified scuba diver, so I concentrated on Tim's directions, not his jokes. Soon, my apprehension gave way to determination, and my breathing slowed to normal. Most of the instruction was done underwater, and because Tim was wearing full scuba gear, he pantomimed diving techniques and used hand signals to convey information. My favorite signal was the one in which the thumb and forefinger formed a circle, and the other three fingers were raised: "Okay!"

At the end of the lesson, Tim climbed out of the pool and announced that we would be putting everything we learned into practice the next day at the beach.

"The beach?" I stepped out of my fins and followed him around the pool deck.

"Yes, we're going on an actual dive," he said, toweling off his shaggy blond hair.

"In the ocean?"

"You didn't think we were going to stay in the pool the whole time, did you?"

Well, yes. I did. That's why I signed up. If the class had been out in the open water that first day, I never would have enrolled. While my classmates laughed at my expense, I tried not to throw up.

Even though I was born and raised in California, the open ocean terrified me. I loved swimming in pools where I could see to the bottom, but when it came to ponds, rivers, lakes, and oceans—especially oceans—I pretty much stayed close to the shore. Something about not being able to see what hid beneath the surface made my skin crawl.

Still, I was in Jamaica, and the inviting waters of the Caribbean Sea gave me an opportunity to get over my irrational fear. But let's face it: even experienced divers had accidents, and I was a total rookie. I aired some of my concerns to Tim.

"It's simple," he said. "If you panic, you drown."

Oh, that made me feel *much* better.

He explained that the scuba experience went against a person's natural instincts. Once below the surface of the water, a novice diver had the tendency to tense up and stop breathing—the opposite of what a diver must do to survive.

A reassuring smile broke across Tim's face. "Just breathe, Barbara, and you'll be fine."

Just breathe. Let go of the anxiety and take a deep breath. Now why hadn't I thought of that?

Nonetheless, I showed up at the beach the next day feeling anxious. No one else seemed to be in my predicament—the other eight students laughed and talked comfortably among themselves. From the bits of their conversation that I overheard, I gathered that they were all attending in pairs. I was the only solo student.

Staring out at the horizon, I evaluated the weather. The ocean looked rough, and dark clouds hung overhead. Maybe I could take a rain check?

"Load up!" Tim called, padding across the sand. "Just watch your step on the deck. It may be a little slippery."

We boarded the boat, and while it sped to the dive site, Tim did a quick refresher course before turning us loose. "It's the same as being in the pool. Only better!"

As the boat slowed, the students began to move into position, cuing up on the dive platform at the stern. Once the boat came to a complete stop, Tim gave the "All clear," our signal to begin launching in pairs. I stalled, ducking to the back of the line, waiting for the others to take their turn. My classmates all stepped into the rough water and floated back to the surface with ease. When it was my turn, my teeth chattered in fear.

Tim put his hands on my shoulders and looked me in the eye. "I know it's raining, Barbara, but it's still like eighty-five degrees out here. You okay?"

"Just relax, right?" I said.

"That's all there is to it. Remember, this is a lazy man's sport!"

I nodded, and together we moved onto the dive platform. With my mouth on my regulator, I confirmed that I was breathing oxygen from the tank. Then, I placed two fingers on my mask and one on my breathing regulator and waited for Tim to give me the signal.

I remembered Grandma Pat's words: "Dive into life, and embrace the joy of uncertainty."

One step later, I was in. I focused on all the things Tim had taught me, taking care not to dwell on my surroundings. If I thought about what might be out there lurking in the water, I might scream, and that would be a disaster.

To my relief, I popped right to the surface. Tim followed me in. We paired up and started a controlled descent to the ocean floor. Although it was turbulent on the surface, the water below was still and quiet. Once I found my buoyancy, I began to drink in the beauty of my surroundings. It wasn't at all murky. I could see everything clearly—and that was the key.

I swam through a brilliant mosaic of reds, yellows, greens, and purples. Primitive sponges shaped like ropes, tubes, baskets, and even elephant ears formed a living structure, a home for brightly striped and spotted fish. A school of moray eels darted beneath the branches of dark green kelp. Fish and rays and dolphins swam around me flashing so many shapes and sizes and colors that it would take a year to learn the names of all the species inhabiting the reef. I saw more marine life in twenty minutes than I had seen in my whole life. The Wiccans had said if you couldn't find God in nature, you'd never find him in a church. I believed God existed there, in the Caribbean Sea. The dive felt like a ceremonial baptism.

Thirty feet below the surface, Tim signaled us to remove our masks and blow out the water. The salt water stung my eyes, but I stayed calm, knowing that my instructor was there with me. Next, Tim signaled for us to remove our breathing regulators and purge the water before replacing them. Then he tapped me on the shoulder to simulate being out of air. I shared my oxygen with him, and we slowly ascended together. The other students followed suit. Thank God I had the instructor as my buddy!

Back at the surface, I finished the emergency exercise by towing Tim back to the boat and pulling his body onto the dive platform. We were the last ones out of the water, and I flung off my mask to give Tim a high five.

"You did it!" he said.

It was hard to believe I'd been afraid to go into the open water. Once I took the plunge, I couldn't wait to go back. Tim took all nine of us on a party cruise to celebrate our newly earned PADI certification. He moored the boat offshore where there was no beach, just rocky cliffs. We took turns scampering up the face then diving into the water. As the sun descended into the sea, we drank potent cocktails and danced the day away. Above the water, now calm and tranquil, the stormy sky had transformed into a showy sunset.

Tim sat down next to me. "Pretty spectacular isn't it?"

"The sunset or the dive?" I asked, spinning the little umbrella around in my drink.

"Both."

"You can keep the sunset, I want to go for another dive." I was filled with desire to explore the ocean, reveling in the fact that I was alive, not just existing.

Tim laughed. "Well, we're doing a night dive on Friday. You should join us."

I didn't respond. My throat grew tight and my hands turned clammy at the thought of diving in the dark.

"It's not so bad," he said. "You thought this afternoon would be scary, and look at you—you're ready to jump back in."

"I don't know …"

"I'll put your name down," he said. "If you can make it, be there. If you can't, don't."

Tim glossed over the milestone of my first dive and seemed bent on hurrying me to the next step. I wanted to savor the moment, not rush headlong toward another challenge. What if I wasn't ready?

—⁂—

When I looked into the water, a liquid sheet of onyx stared back at me. I felt small standing in the still air beneath the countless pinpricks of light that lit up the sky. Even though the sound of the water lapping against the boat's bow comforted me, I longed for the visual reassurance of watching the gentle rollers.

As Tim went over the procedures, I noticed that none of the members from the beginner's group were in the boat, which made me more than a little nervous. Tim explained that the night dive wasn't much different from a daytime dive, except we'd be using flashlights. We were near the ruins of a sunken ship, about five miles south of where I had lost my scuba virginity a few days before.

I felt nauseous, but I knew it wasn't seasickness. It was my nerves. So many things could go wrong. What if the light attracted curious sea creatures, hungry for a midnight snack? Even worse, what if I got lost? Worst of all, what if I dropped my flashlight?

I tried to clear my head of any negativity and instead concentrated on Tim's words. He said we'd all launch from the ship together, and we weren't allowed to go off exploring by ourselves. The buddy system was mandatory. He didn't crack any sex jokes this time.

There were ten of us in the group, and we gave each other tentative nods as we readied ourselves for the dive. We got the cue from Tim, and like a team of synchronized swimmers, we plunged into the deep. The beams from our flashlights danced in the water as we waved them around to get our bearings. The flashlights were adjustable, and I learned that by twisting the head, I could change the focus of light from a wide angle to a narrow beam. Even though the narrow beam lit up a smaller space, I preferred its intensity to the dimmer wide angle of light, which had a backscatter effect that made it difficult to see.

Tim was wrong. The night dive was much different from a daytime dive—it was even more breathtakingly gorgeous. Though I couldn't see nearly as far—only ten feet in front of me—the brilliant colors I remembered from my daytime dive were even sharper and more vivid at night. The colors of the marine life lit up the underworld like Las Vegas neon. My flashlight really did attract curious creatures. Fish swam right up to me, but instead of being nervous, I felt at ease in the calm that settled over the underwater scene.

Tim guided us toward the sunken ship we'd come to see. A school of eels drifted by, and we caught some sea slugs mating. I wondered what Tim would have to say about that. The ship lay wedged on her side, her once-proud bow mottled by age and slick with algae. Pushing through one of the many gaping holes, we saw two giant sea turtles, side by side, on what had probably been the upper deck. Red crabs skittered sideways along the corroded metal, and a furry green moss wrapped around the railings. That ship had once sailed the Caribbean Sea. Years later, she rested on the ocean floor, transformed into an artificial reef and a haven for sea life.

I wondered what had sunk the ship and looked for the remnants of a lifeboat. Visions of the movies *Poseidon Adventure* and *The Titanic* flashed through my mind. I imagined I could hear the whispers of the ship's former passengers, but I couldn't tell what they were saying.

Brushing my morbid thoughts aside, I focused on the beauty of the sea and my role in taking care of it so it didn't share the same fate as the sunken ship—a wreck for future generations to explore and wonder where it all went wrong.

It seemed like only a few minutes had passed when Tim signaled for us to return to the boat. I stole one last glance at the spooky ship and looked upward, paddling my way to the surface. My mask broke through with a soft splash.

When we returned to shore, I took a deep breath and let out a relieved sigh. The night dive had been a big step for me. I'd faced my fears and conquered them, a pattern I intended to follow.

Chapter 16

THE ROAD LESS TRAVELED

The next day, I went to the concierge's desk and inquired about horseback riding. I wanted to get out and explore the countryside, just as I'd done in Ireland. Although I had enjoyed almost a week of hedonism, sunning on the beach during the day and dancing deep into the night, I found the sexually charged atmosphere somewhat stressful. The more people told me to "relax" or "go with the flow," the more uptight I became. The scuba lessons were a welcome distraction from the nonstop eroticism. While I wasn't quite ready to throw in the towel and admit it wasn't the lifestyle for me, I wanted to get away from the resort for a few hours and clear my head.

The concierge provided the name of a nearby stable and called a cab. I heard the vehicle long before I saw it—an awful, sputtering clunker that sounded like a smoker coughing. The mustard-yellow taxi wheezed to a stop in front of the resort. Held together by duct tape and bailing wire, it looked as bad as it sounded and smelled even worse. When the driver rolled down his window, I nearly gagged at the stench—a sickening combination of ganja and wet dog.

"Can you take me to the stable?" I asked.

The driver smiled, flashing a gold tooth. "Oh, yeah, mon. Climb in!"

"Is it far?" I asked, not sure how long I could hold my breath. "Do you think we'll make it?"

"Don't mind the noise. My car is very reliable, mon."

I got into the rear seat of the cab, scooting forward as far as possible in an attempt to minimize my contact with the decrepit upholstery. The interior door handle was missing, so I rolled down the window and pulled the door closed.

While a thin trickle of sweat slithered down my back, I fanned myself with my hat and tried not to inhale the taxi's wretched odor. We drove down the coast, winding through several small parishes, each more rundown than the last. Rasta colors lined the streets. The huts were splashed in hues of yellow, red, and green. Some of the shanties were little more than shelters with vinyl tarps tacked onto splintered wood. I smiled when I saw the bright African tulips soaring into the sky amidst dirty buckets used to collect rainwater. A chatter of honking horns assaulted my ears as we passed roadside stands selling apples and ackee, a fruit originally transported to Jamaica from West Africa.

Young girls in the streets giggled as they bounced to reggae music, trying out new moves for the amusement of their friends, and shirtless boys picked tunes on guitars that were missing tuning pegs and strings. A group of barefoot children made a game of kicking soccer balls up and over the lines of drying laundry. The driver slowed considerably as we rolled through the villages, and I welcomed the scent of the Jamaican spices when we passed an open barbecue strewn with jerk chicken. My stomach started to growl.

"It looks like the villagers built these houses themselves," I said.

"Yeah, they did. They have no money, so they have to be creative. A scrap here, a scrap there. Build a house piece by piece that way."

Going from a luxurious beach resort to these humble parishes, I felt a pang of guilt. Because the resort was all-inclusive, the buffets were stocked right up to the end of the meal. I'd wondered what happened to all the food that disappeared into the kitchen once the mealtime ended. Did the staff just throw it away? It would've been a shame. An entire parish could eat for a week on that food. The taxi driver seemed to read my thoughts.

"People who live here don't need much. They live off the land, grow their own crops, raise chickens and goats. Their home is in God's garden."

For the first time, I thought about the way a house can separate a person from the rest of the world, how a structure can become a world of its own, leaving its occupants unaware of the greater beauty that lies beyond its doors. We slowed to a crawl as we came upon a small group of children clearing rocks from the road. As the driver braked, the children ran over and surrounded us, their dirty hands pushing through my open window.

"What do they want?" I asked. I could feel the panic creeping up my neck.

"They're harmless," the driver said. I heard the sound of loose coins as he fished around in his ashtray. "They're just trying to make a little money. The road needs repair, and they're keeping us from getting a flat tire."

He rolled down his window and threw a couple of coins their way. I don't know if he did it out of generosity or just to get the kids away from my window, but I appreciated the gesture.

"Wait a minute," I said as the taxi rolled forward. I reached into my purse and came up with some Jamaican bills. I called to the children and thrust my hand out the window. They scurried back to the taxi and snatched the money as if they were afraid I might change my mind.

"Thank you, friend!" they shouted before running off.

"That was very kind, mon," the driver said.

I shook my head and looked out the rear window. "It was nothing."

I'd given away two hundred Jamaica dollars, about two US dollars. I don't know why, but I suddenly felt foolish. Did I give too little?

Or did my first-world guilt make me an even uglier American than I already was? Textbook tourism: damned if you do, damned if you don't. I resigned myself to the shabby upholstery and sat back in the frayed seat; then I closed my eyes and did my best to keep the stench from overwhelming me.

A loud boom interrupted my reverie. The taxi lurched, and I reached for the missing door handle.

"What was that?" I asked.

"Nothing." The taxi lugged along in an unsettling motion.

"It didn't sound like 'nothing.'" I reached through my open window and gripped the handle from the outside, ready to flee.

"Everything's good," the driver said, flashing his gold tooth in an unconvincing smile in the rearview mirror. The disturbed look in his eyes told another story.

I shot back to the edge of my seat when another loud noise rumbled through the taxi. That time, I could tell the sound had come from under the vehicle's hood. The car shuddered and came to a stop in the middle of the road. The last parish we'd passed through was at least a mile behind us.

The driver unleashed a colorful string of what sounded like profanities. He tried to start the taxi but nothing happened. He tried again and again, but the engine refused to turn over.

"Are we stranded?"

The driver got out of the taxi to look around, and I did the same. We were at the bottom of a steep, dusty hill. At the crown stood a large building surrounded by rickety structures bound together with sheets of corrugated metal.

"We going to have to go for help, mon."

"Can't you radio for assistance?" My heart pounded as I recalled my sisters' words of caution about traveling alone.

The driver shook his head. "When I break down, they just tell me to go get help."

I was not encouraged by the way he said "when" instead of "if." This probably wasn't the first time his chariot had choked.

"Can we call someone? Do you have a cell phone?"

"The cell phone is too much for me," he said, shaking his head.

There wasn't a whole lot I could say to that. A man who gave his spare change to beggars couldn't afford his own phone. I couldn't imagine leaving the house without a cell phone, much less operating a taxi. I automatically reached into my purse to offer him mine, but it wasn't there. I had left the resort without it. My impulsiveness had gotten the best of me again.

"We go up there," the driver said. "I bet they can help."

A dark ring of sweat showed under his arm when he pointed to the building at the top of the hill. He started up the road. I followed.

We marched past makeshift homes. Rasta men drinking Red Stripe watched us pass. I breathed in the familiar scent of weed, pervasive in the Jamaican air. Laughing children collected water from the streams using recycled plastic bottles, and uniformed schoolgirls offered cheerful "hellos." The sun was blazing, and without the ocean breeze, I was soon drenched in sweat. My T-shirt stuck to me, uncomfortably plastered to my damp skin. As we labored up the hill, dodging stray dogs and wild goats, the driver's short-sleeved polo turned from bright red to a deep shade of maroon.

Near the top, a cluster of young men dressed in tattered shorts and threadbare tank tops huddled around a small roadside fire, which popped bright sparks into the street. The acrid odor of whatever they were cooking stung my nostrils, and the greasy smoke hung in the humid air. I didn't see how they could stand it. I felt dizzy and light-headed and was utterly unprepared for their taunts.

"Can I be the lucky mon?"

"You like the big bamboo?"

"Me can lock me hose off!"

"Leave the lady alone!" the driver growled.

I was too frightened to respond. I wasn't sure my driver could hold his own against the young men, so I looked away, avoiding eye contact with them. The dance floor at Hedo had given me a taste of how forward Jamaican men could be. They seemed to enjoy competing with each other while trying to attract attention from females. Any attention—good or bad—was better than none at all, it seemed. But we were far from the safe enclosure of the resort, and their cocky banter felt threatening. Thankfully, we arrived at the gates of the building we had spotted from below.

We stood at the entrance, trying to catch our breath. A crumpled chain-link fence topped with barbed wire surrounded the entire property. The gate was closed with a length of rusty chain and padlocked shut. I was panting from the hike and the heat. I no longer cared about the taxi. All I wanted was a drink of water.

"Now what do we do?" I asked. Somehow, I thought he would have a solution.

The driver pointed to a hole in the fence, just large enough to sneak through. I didn't want to risk the ire of whoever had gone through so much trouble to keep people out, but I didn't want to walk past the young men again either.

"I don't want to trespass."

The driver threw up his hands, then cupped them around his mouth and started shouting for help.

That surprised me. Was our situation really so dire? I joined in his calls, and we both stood there yelling through the chain-link fence, hoping someone would hear us. Eventually, a plump woman with copper-colored skin and wiry black hair waddled out.

"What all this screaming for? What you want?" she hissed.

"My taxi broke down at the bottom of the hill, ma'am, and I need to call for help. Can I please use your phone?" the driver asked. The woman eyed us suspiciously.

"Please, ma'am," I said, "we'll only be a minute."

The woman grunted and withdrew a massive key ring from her pocket. There must have been fifty keys looped together. She unlocked the gate, pulled it open, and waved us in. We rushed inside and huddled in the shade.

"Thank you so much," I said.

"Yeah, yeah," she muttered as she ushered us toward the main building.

The compound was much larger than it looked from the road. Outbuildings in various stages of construction surrounded the main structure. "Is this a school?" I asked.

"More than that."

The woman raised a thick arm and pointed to a sign that read, "The Windsor Girls Home." I hadn't noticed it when we first walked up.

"The girls live here so they can get off the streets. Most of them have no other place to go."

She led us inside to an administrative office that had an institutional feel. The air was hot and stale, and the lone ceiling fan did little to chase away the heat. The walls were gray from years of dirt and grime, and the wooden floors were warped unevenly.

The woman showed the driver to the phone. It was an old-fashioned rotary phone, and it took the taxi driver several tries before he was able to get through to an operator. Sensing that things might take a while, I asked the woman her name.

"Shamara." She smiled with surprising sweetness. "Come on, I'll give you the grand tour." Maybe she decided I wasn't a threat to her girls, and as she took my arm, I let my guard down a notch, too. We headed outside, and I asked her about the barbed-wire fence.

"It's not to keep the girls in," she said. "It's to keep the men out. They are always trying to lure the girls into prostitution."

"Prostitution? Is it legal here?"

"No, it's not legal, but the law's not enforced either, especially with the tourists."

The fence made the place feel like a prison in reverse: all the criminals were on the outside. I told Shamara about the hole in the fence, and how we'd considered crawling through. She squinted at me and wiped the sweat from her forehead with the back of her hand. A dozen bangles slid down her arm and rattled together with a tinny clink.

"I know all about that, and it's a good thing you didn't try to crawl through. I would have let the dogs on you." The hair on my arms went up at the thought of being chased down by feral dogs. I felt vindicated by my earlier concern about trespassing.

"What about the girls' families?" I asked, stepping around a pile of crumbled cinderblocks.

"The families that these girls come from are very poor. Drug-addicted mothers sell their daughters into prostitution. Fathers and uncles have their way with daughters and nieces who are still just little girls." Shamara adjusted the woven scarf she wore on her head. She spoke frankly, but the shocking reality of the girls' screwed-up family life still seemed to get under her skin.

"That's so sad." As a mother, I couldn't imagine this type of behavior, even if I were destitute, and I would cut the balls off any man who tried to rape one of my daughters.

"The girls who end up on the streets aren't bad, just starved for love," Shamara said. "All they really want is a little attention, but because they were raised without self-esteem, they end up selling themselves as prostitutes or getting abused, thinking they have no other choice. I give them a choice."

Shamara steered me around the orphanage. Her sour attitude had disappeared, but our brief conversation had given some validity to the defensive demeanor with which she had greeted us at the gate. As we got acquainted, I could see how she'd be good with the "bad girls" of the Windsor Girls Home.

She took me through the classroom, sewing room, kitchen, and a tiny lab where there were eight computers for sixty girls. The rooms were little more than old bedrooms converted into teaching areas. Shamara introduced me to the other workers—dorm counselors and teachers—who smiled at me warily. Tourists didn't visit the Windsor Girls Home.

A bell rang, and the corridor filled with a jumble of girls in all shapes and sizes—big and tall with long arms and spindly legs, round and small with chubby legs and thick arms. Acne pocked the faces of some, while the complexions of others shone smooth and flawless. A throng of girls with gap-toothed grins swarmed around me, reaching for my hair, tugging at the sleeve of my shirt, petting my arm as if I were a cat. At first, the attention startled me, then I felt overwhelmed by so many hands reaching for me. I soon found myself caught up in the girl's euphoria and giggled along with them. Shamara had been right. These girls were starving for affection.

"Look how they crowd around you!" Shamara laughed. "It's like you're a queen!"

"Will you be our mom?" one of the girls asked.

"What do I do?" I asked Shamara. I looked at her across the crowded corridor, seeking guidance.

"Just be yourself, girl."

I recalled the days when my two daughters were very young and they both wanted my attention at the same time. It felt like that—times thirty. I asked the girls their names and their ages and told them how pretty they were.

After a few minutes, Shamara broke up the mob. "Who's hungry?" she asked.

The hallway filled with a chorus of girls shouting "Me!" in unison.

"Wanna help?" Shamara asked me. "I could use a hand getting lunch together."

"Just tell me what you need," I said.

"Follow me!" As if on cue, two girls grabbed my hands, while others trailed behind. They seemed afraid to leave my side, lest I disappear.

The taxi driver was waiting in the kitchen, probably wondering where we had been. He appeared uncomfortable there, surrounded by so many girls, and nervously ran a hand over his balding head.

"Did you get through?" I asked.

"Yes, but the vehicle can't be towed until later. They can send another taxi right away." I suppressed a little chortle, knowing that nothing happens "right away" in Jamaica. Everyone lives on island time.

The girls on either side of me let go of my hands. They backed away, silent and despondent. I could sense the disappointment in all of the girls, not just the ones who had been holding my hands. Was I being ridiculous? I'd only met them a few minutes earlier, but I didn't want to let them down.

"We have to make lunch first," I said.

"No problem," said the driver. "We can call back any time. I'll wait here until the tow truck shows up."

And without a second thought, I committed to spending the day at the Windsor Girls Home. The girls cheered, and though Shamara told them to hush, I could tell she was as pleased as they were.

Chapter 17

PRISON IN PARADISE

Like everything else at the Windsor Girls Home, the dark kitchen was cramped and crowded. A small, padlocked refrigerator rested against the back wall. Pots and pans filled the sink, and wooden cutting boards—scarred like grooved records—leaned up against a rusty metal cabinet. On the back burner of the gas stove, something simmered in a black pot, filling the room with an aroma of exotic spices whose origin I could not pinpoint. Shamara handed me a faded apron.

"What are we making?" I asked, as I tied the apron around my waist.

"Boiled bananas and cassava. Have you had it?"

The banana part was obvious, but I had never heard of cassava. "I don't even know what that is!"

Shamara went to the refrigerator and began assembling ingredients on the small counter next to the sink.

"Cassava is a plant. We eat the root. It's like a yam or sweet potato. We eat curry goat, too. You've had that, right?"

"No. Just goat cheese." I was embarrassed by my culinary naïveté. Even through I had mastered cooking like Betty Crocker, I was sadly inexperienced when it came to rudimentary ethnic ingredients, aside from those I used in my paella.

"You got to get out more, girl," said Shamara, with an exasperated roll of her eyes. "Here in Jamaica we eat a lot of goat. We eat the hooves, the intestines, even the head."

"You're kidding me!"

"I'm not. We make goat-head soup. It's one of my favorites."

Two of the older girls who were helping in the kitchen nodded their heads enthusiastically. For the next hour, we chopped vegetables and stirred them into steaming pots. The spicy scent of cinnamon, cloves, and red pepper wafted through the kitchen. Even though we cooked with strange ingredients, I felt at home—comfortable with Shamara and her girls. To drink, we mixed up jugs of tart limeade made from freshly squeezed limes and sweetened with cane sugar.

At Shamara's command, the girls assembled outdoors on cracked plastic chairs crammed around stained tables. On the back wall of the covered cafeteria, a mural painted in bright yellows, blues, and greens depicted the Virgin Mary keeping a watchful eye over the girls. I was drawn to the figure in the mural. Like Mona Lisa, the Virgin Mary had eyes that seemed to follow me wherever I went.

I thought of how the Wiccans respected Mary, and how the pilgrims had prayed to her at Knock. She was the only female role model in modern Christianity, but my Baptist upbringing had attempted to banish her. I was happy to see her watching over us at the Windsor Girls Home.

Shamara and I assembled the lunch plates and brought them outside. The girls eagerly grabbed the plates, hinting at the scarcity of food they might have grown up with. Once we had served every girl, we picked up our own plates and joined them, already halfway through their meals, at an old Formica-covered table.

Shamara dug into her lunch with gusto, and I followed her lead. Rich meat dripped with oily sauce; tangy herbs and fiery spices laced the mashed root vegetables. The goat was fork-tender, the red peas had a buttery texture, and the rice had kick that got my attention. Shamara was right about the cassava—it tasted a lot like a sweet potato. I ate as if I hadn't eaten for days, savoring each bite. I enjoyed our humble lunch more than any meal I'd had at the resort, where I ate quickly, afraid some naked man would sit next to me with his frank and beans on display.

"Are you enjoying your vacation?" Shamara asked.

"It's been nice," I said. "Nice" was one of those words like "interesting." I used it when I wanted to be polite, if not completely honest.

Shamara raised her eyebrows. It seemed as if she could sense my discontent.

"Well, it's not exactly what I was expecting. I mean the hotel is amazing and everything, but I wanted to see more of the island, the people. When I decided to get out and explore a bit, the taxi broke down, and now, here I am." I looked around at the resident girls and the simple spread. "Listen to me, complaining about my vacation when ..." I stopped abruptly, silenced by a loss for words.

I scanned the grounds beyond the cafeteria, searching for something besides Shamara to focus my attention on, but the structures of the Windsor Girls Home blurred into a single wall and the dense jungle foliage blended into the background. At the long dining tables, coarse black cornrows sprouted from innocent heads that probably already knew too much.

"The girls really appreciate your being here, and if you run out of things to do out there," Shamara said with a nod, indicating the world beyond the fence, "we could use your help here."

The wide eyes of the girl seated next to me stared up at me with a silent plea. Without looking away, she brought another forkful of curry to her mouth.

"Really?" The change in Shamara's attitude made me feel more like an overdue visitor than an unexpected intruder. "Doing what?"

"You could teach the girls English and math." The girl beside me nodded while she chewed her food, pausing to gulp down some limeade.

"But I'm not a teacher!"

"Any of us can teach when we are needed," Shamara said. "I didn't come here as a teacher either, but now I couldn't imagine my life any other way." She crossed the cafeteria to where her tote bag hung from the back of a chair, withdrew a stack of papers, and handed them to me. Quickly flipping through the pages, I realized that teaching these girls wouldn't be hard at all. The reading comprehension exercises looked to be about a second-grade reading level back in the States. I could tell that the girls were already intrigued by me. I was a lost white woman, stranded inside their prison yet willing to stay. Who was I? Good question.

"Come on, there are a few girls I want you to meet." Shamara led me to a nearby table. "Barbara, meet Monique."

Shamara sat down and gave the girl a hug. The girl smiled. Her two front teeth were missing, and her white blouse was blotchy with stains. A concave dip marred her forehead, and the rest of her face bore jagged scars.

I knelt down and held out my hand. "Hi, how are you?"

"Fine," she whispered, but didn't take my hand. Her eyes drilled into the cafeteria floor.

"Monique is thirteen," Shamara explained. "She's been here a year and wants to be a photographer."

"Really? I have a camera in my purse."

Shamara leaned over to me and lowered her voice. "Don't offer to take her picture. The only time she's ever had her picture taken was for pornographic purposes."

I felt the color drain from my face as Shamara shared that information. "I'll be right back," I said, excusing myself. With unsteady strides, I crossed the cafeteria, breathing deeply to restore the flow of oxygen to my head. Inside the stuffy kitchen, I retrieved the camera from my purse and took a moment to freshen my makeup and regain my composure. When I returned to the table, I sat next to Monique, leaving a wide buffer between us. I didn't want to frighten her by encroaching on her space.

Without a word, Monique extended a shaky hand toward my camera. Her other hand remained tightly clamped around Shamara's. I handed her the camera and watched her examine the little silver machine, fascinated by the black screen and the tiny buttons. The wonder with which she explored the camera tugged at my heart.

"Would you like to take my picture?" I asked. "You can be the photographer." I reached over and turned the camera on. "Look through the screen, and then push this button when you're ready," I explained.

"Can Monique take my picture?" A skinny girl with a bold smile pushed her way between Monique and me, resting a sticky hand on my knee. "I've never had my picture taken."

Her simple statement took my breath away. I thought of the thousands of photos I'd taken of my girls from the time they were babies. Each one was a symbol of my love for them, an expression of my desire to keep them in my heart forever. It was an experience this girl had never had, not even once.

"Go ahead, Monique," I urged. The skinny girl took a few steps back, then cocked her hips to one side.

Monique lined up her shot. "Smile, Marsha," she instructed. Marsha struck a series of poses for Monique as if she were a veteran model or a glamorous rock star.

"You said you'd never had your picture taken," I teased, amazed at how charismatic she was.

"I'm pretending to be Beyoncé," Marsha said in between shots. "She's always having her picture taken."

The environment in which these Jamaican girls grew up couldn't have been more different from the one in which my daughters were raised, but they all knew the same popular singer. No matter how different their daily lives, teenage girls around the world were just that. Teenage girls.

Monique brought the camera back to me, and I switched it into playback mode. The girls crowded around to look at the photographs, marveling that they could see themselves inside the camera. I flipped the switch back to camera mode, and within a matter of minutes, Monique was confidently snapping pictures again. Each girl wanted to be next. While Monique cued up her subjects, Marsha moved her chair closer to mine, slipped her hand through the crook of my elbow, and laid her head on my shoulder.

"You remind me of my mama," she said softly.

I felt a hot tear run down my face. Right then, I wanted to be her mother—I wanted to be a mother to every one of those girls. I understood how Sister Catherine felt when she described her maternal bond to the young sisters who joined the order. Marsha sat there, quietly nestled against my arm, until the loud scrape of Shamara's chair roused her as the dark, full-figured woman pushed back from the table.

"I'll go see if Monique needs any help," Shamara said. "You and Marsha take some time to get to know each other. Marsha, tell Barbara what you do here."

Marsha waited until Shamara was gone before she sat up and announced that she was in charge of the goat.

"I walk the goat out by the main road and tie him to a tree for the day to eat all the grass." Her eyes were bright, and the smile had returned to her face, smooth and radiant with youth. While she talked, Marsha pulled down on the shirt that hung loosely on her thin frame. Her bony knees jutted out from beneath her shorts, and her toes curled around a pair of worn flip-flops that were too big for her little feet.

"Aren't you afraid someone will steal your goat if you leave him by the road all day?" I asked.

She snorted with laughter. "No. You get in worse trouble for stealing a goat than you do for rape."

The frank admission by a girl so young shocked me into silence.

Another girl joined us at the table. She had a tall, lithe body and big, dark eyes. "Tell me your name," she demanded.

I was a little taken aback by the girl's blunt demeanor, yet it was clear that she carried herself with confidence. "Barbara. And yours?" I asked.

"My name is Naomi. You staying all day?"

"Yes," I said, eyeing the stack of papers Shamara had left for me to correct. "I believe so."

Naomi gave a sharp nod. "Good. I'm in charge of the chickens." She pointed a few yards away to a coop. The patch of grass that surrounded it was filled with chicks that would someday grow into hens. "You can help me feed them tonight."

"You got it," I said.

Naomi smiled, pleased with my decision. I didn't believe that Naomi really wanted me to help with her chickens. It was her cagey way of finding out how long I planned to stay.

Monique had come back to the table, anxious to show me the pictures she'd taken. A few minutes later, Shamara tapped me on the shoulder. She still wore an apron around her thick middle and held a dishtowel in her hand.

"The girls have class now. You can help with the dishes, if you like."

I realized I'd become something of a distraction, a disruption to the routine of girls who needed a reliable schedule. "Come on," I said. "You heard Shamara. Time for school."

The girls groaned. Monique reluctantly handed me the camera, and Marsha's scrawny shoulders sagged.

"Oh, come on now. When you're done with class, we'll play."

"You promise?" Naomi asked, her eyes searching mine for a finite commitment.

"I promise," I said.

The girls pulled away from me and trudged toward their classrooms.

I could tell they didn't believe me. They had probably heard their share of empty promises.

I helped Shamara gather up the dishes, and we headed inside. The kitchen felt like a sauna. Shamara filled the chipped sink and began to pile dirty dishes in the scalding water. Outside the kitchen door, a pair of scraggly mutts lay stretched out on the mottled brown grass. Shamara tossed some leftovers their way, and the dogs got up to devour every scrap before collapsing again in the hot grass.

"Can you tell me a little more about the girls?" I asked.

"What do you want to know?" She plunged her arms into the soapy water.

"Like how they came to be here. Tell me about Monique."

Shamara heaved a big sigh and started to methodically scrub the dishes. All the girls were back in the classroom, and I got the impression that doing dishes helped Shamara relax. She looked weary and overworked.

"You sure you want to know?"

"Yes," I said as I wiped down the countertops. I'm not sure why I asked. I suppose I was just making conversation, trying to learn more about the place while I helped Shamara with the chores. I reflected on the change that had come over Monique during the afternoon, how she had gone from terribly shy to triumphantly confident. I had assumed I could help her, and that it would all be as easy as handing her a camera to play with. But I learned that there was more to it.

Shamara explained that Monique's mother died while giving birth. With no other family, baby Monique was handed over to an orphanage. When she was ten, she ran away and was lured into prostitution. One of her "customers" bashed her face in, knocking out her front teeth. When I had first seen Monique, I had imagined her disfigured face was caused by a childhood accident, not by blatant brutality. My stomach turned, and I felt a rush of anger. Shamara went on to tell me that Monique was later turned over to social services, which decided that her only option was the Windsor Girls Home.

The pile of washed dishes grew as I fell behind on my drying duties. "Should I go on?" Shamara asked. I nodded.

She moved to Marsha, Monique's roommate, who had been raped by one of her uncles. Afraid to tell anyone for fear she'd catch the blame, Marsha ran away from home. To get by, she sold seashell necklaces to the tourists on the beach. The most she ever made in one day selling jewelry was five dollars. I felt a sudden rush of guilt. I spent that much on a daily cup of coffee that I almost never finished. The relative value of five dollars was so obvious when viewed from that perspective. My brain started spinning with ideas of how I might be able to change these girls' lives.

Shamara pulled the plug in the sink, and the dishwater began to drain as she described Naomi—the only girl of six children. Her mother had died and her father worked as a farmer in a small parish. Naomi came to Windsor because she had been abused and bullied. At school, she was often involved in fights. Other kids threw bleach and eggs at her. She hoped to go live with her aunt when she left Windsor.

I stopped drying dishes and grasped the counter to steady myself. "Oh, my gosh," I whispered, my eyes welling up. "Now I understand why the girls asked me to be their mom."

Shamara went on to tell me more stories about the kinds of trouble the girls could get into and how the government was more hindrance than help.

"Some of the girls sneak out at night to meet men who are waiting at the gate or at the hole you saw in the fence. Sometimes, the girls disappear for days. We know they are sexually active, but it's illegal to give minors birth control."

"What about condoms?" Shamara laughed at my naiveté as she stowed the large pot we'd used to cook our soup.

"It doesn't work that way here, lady. Condoms mean you're dirty. Unclean."

"So what happens when the girls get pregnant?" I asked.

"We send them to another home during their pregnancy. After they give birth, the girls return to Windsor where some keep spinning a vicious cycle, becoming pregnant again because they are so desperate for love and attention. We place the babies in an orphanage, where they are raised until they are eighteen."

I shook my head. The girls endured extreme poverty, rampant abuse, and blatant exploitation. In some cases, their mothers had allowed them to be mistreated by their fathers. Did their lack of strength and conviction make them responsible for their husbands' actions? If any husband of mine were physically abusing my children or me, I'd muster the strength to take a stand. I said a silent prayer of thanks for the safe and loving environment in which my daughters were raised.

The girls at Windsor had limited education and employment options, so the outlook for their future was bleak. What chance did they have for a productive life outside the fence?

"I've been so fortunate because I had choices," I began, "but these girls ..."

Shamara dried her hands and arranged the dishtowels on the edge of the sink to dry.

"Barbara, sometimes that's just the way it is. Even though I'm a native Jamaican, I was lucky enough to have choices, too. And I got a pretty good education. Sometimes, the best thing we can do is show these girls that possibilities exist."

"But how?"

"By being an example. By showing them that they don't have to settle for the streets. They can have a home, an education, a career. These girls need to learn that if a woman has an education, she has choices."

It was sweltering in that kitchen, but my discomfort had nothing to do with the heat. Part of me wanted to flee all that squalor and depression, call the taxi to take me horseback riding. I once read that half of the world's population makes a wage of two dollars a day. At the time, I'd glossed over the galling statistic, but the price of a cup of coffee or a newspaper was a lifeline to a better future for girls like Monique, Marsha, and Naomi. I'd been blessed with so many opportunities— opportunities these girls would never have.

"I want to help, but what difference could I possibly make?

"Most of these girls will never get to live the life they want," Shamara said, taking my hand in hers. "Life's not fair, but one hand washes the other. We've got to help each other. That's the only way we can help ourselves."

"But that's not the reason I'm here," I started to protest, but Shamara wouldn't hear a word of it.

"As soon as I laid eyes on you I thought, 'This girl is searching for something.'" She patted my hand in a way that my grandmother might.

"Is it that obvious?" I asked.

"Spend the night with us," she said. "You just might find it."

Chapter 18

CHOICES

As tired as I was from the day's labors, I couldn't sleep. Although my accommodations were far less luxurious than the resort, the lumpy mattress and threadbare sheets in the dorm room I shared with four other girls had nothing to do with my restlessness. Shamara's stories about the girls' backgrounds disturbed me. I had also learned some unsettling details about the home itself.

Prior to its conversion to an orphanage, the Windsor Girls Home was one of the most highly regarded tourist hotels in Saint Ann's Bay. By the time the social services took it over, squatters had subverted the neighborhood into an area that had the sixth highest number of teen and preteen pregnancies on the island. Where vacationers once strolled, young girls worked as prostitutes. The government spent over one million dollars a year on perimeter security at the Windsor Girls Home. Money that should have been dedicated to the girls was being spent on failed attempts to keep the predators out.

I tossed and turned, hot and sticky in my tattered nightshirt. Since I didn't have a nightgown, or even a spare T-shirt, I had to borrow a torn white shirt from a bag of clothes in the sewing room. I mended it on the old machine. My ability to sew was another one of Grandma Pat's gifts. Since the skill had served her so well both on and off the vaudeville stage, she'd insisted that I learn the basics. I had a knack for the hobby and became an accomplished seamstress, passing the skill along to my daughters. I'd shown Naomi a bit about sewing while I mended my nightshirt, and Shamara had watched with an amused expression.

Lying in bed, I listened to my "roommates" giggling with one another until the soothing sound of deep breathing replaced their laughter. Though the room was quiet, I could still hear the faint strains of reggae in the night and imagined it came from a radio belonging to one of the men who lurked outside the gate. It made me angry, and I wanted to creep down the hill in my white nightshirt and scare them away like a vengeful ghost.

While I understood that the bars on the windows were for the girls' safety, on that night they filled me with anxiety and made me feel like a prisoner. What if there was a fire? How would we get out? After a few minutes of letting my thoughts run wild, I calmed down and chided myself. I could leave anytime, but the girls were stuck there. It seemed so unfair, so difficult to reconcile. What right did I have to such excess when they struggled to meet their basic needs? It was confusing and overwhelming, like trying to solve an equation on a blackboard that stretched as far as the eye could see. If I figured out what I was looking at or erased it to make the problem go away, there were still miles of slate to go.

The color of my skin and the country of my passport separated me from the girls. Those two things gave me freedom and opportunity. Even though I wasn't ever physically or sexually abused like those girls, I did know that when a woman loses her voice, she suffers indignity.

Unlike those girls, I'd found acceptance and love, but I'd had to wear a mask to gain that acceptance and receive that love. Without realizing it, I'd played the role of the good girl and hidden my true self all my life. Afraid of being rejected by my family and my friends, I had locked away my secrets, along with my soul. Staring up at the gray ceiling at the Windsor Girls Home, watching the lazy twirl of the fan,

I knew the exact moment when I had set foot inside the gilded cage and swallowed the key.

———✳———

It was my senior year of college. I was finishing up my physical therapy internships and getting ready to graduate. Jay had already begun a promising home-building career. We'd been dating for three years, and although premarital sex went against my religious upbringing, I was in love and would do anything for my future husband. I had been raised to believe it was a sin to lose my virginity out of wedlock, but since we would soon be married, I gave in to my desires. My hormones got the best of me, but I didn't fight it. I wanted to show Jay that I loved him.

Then, just before our wedding, I missed my period.

Even though we had intercourse regularly, I thought going on birth control would be an open admission that I had discovered sex. Of course in hindsight, admitting I was on the pill would have been far easier than admitting I was off my monthly schedule.

Jay and I sat at a small table draped with a red-checked tablecloth in our favorite Italian restaurant. Raffia-wrapped Chianti bottles hung from the ceiling. We had both ordered lasagna. I took a gulp of water and repositioned the breadbasket, imagining how I might tell him.

"I'm late."

"For what?" he'd ask, refilling his wine glass and eying mine, untouched.

"You know, my period."

"I thought girls were late all the time. Late for class, late for dinner. Why should this be any different?" He would smile and wink at me.

I couldn't tell him until I knew for sure. Maybe I really was just late, not pregnant. I fidgeted with the stem of my wine glass and swirled the illicit liquid that pushed the boundaries of my upbringing and raised a forbidden flag for pregnant women.

Too ashamed to tell my girlfriends and not about to ask the women in my family for help—not even Grandma Pat—I looked up Planned Parenthood in the yellow pages. When I found it, I stared at the number for four solid hours before I got up the nerve to call for an appointment. I told myself it was just like scheduling a routine checkup or a teeth cleaning. Except it wasn't.

On the day of my appointment, I walked into the clinic, frightened and alone. The counselor immediately took my hand and embraced me with a warm hug, seeming to know how difficult my situation was. She reached out to me in a way that no one else could. Unlike me, she had seen this all before. She wrapped me in tenderness and understanding when I had no one else to confide in. Through it all, she was sensitive and caring—right up until the moment when I lay on the table with my legs spread wide and tears running down my face.

"The test came back negative, and your pelvic exam was normal," she said.

I couldn't talk through the tears. I was so relieved. I loved Jay, and I wanted to have his children. But not then. Neither one of us was ready.

I hadn't asked him to come with me to see the counselor or be there during the exam. I was the one who might have been pregnant, and dealing with it was my responsibility. By having unprotected sex, I'd made a mistake—a huge mistake.

In the days and weeks that followed, I slid into a silent sadness. Someone more clinical might say I was depressed. I wondered about the life that might have been inside me. But if I had been pregnant, the timing would have been all wrong.

If I had dropped out of college to have a baby, it would have significantly limited my options later in life. I knew my education was the key to my independence, despite my plan to marry Jay. I would have struggled mightily with the choice between giving a child up and quitting school. I had never thought about the difficulty of deciding between abortion or adoption, though I understood that part of being a woman was having the freedom of choice. When I finally did become a mother, I taught my daughters how to take responsibility for their bodies and how avoid one of the most difficult decisions a woman could ever make.

---~~~---

I lay in bed in the rustic dormitory, unable to sleep, thinking about the girls at Windsor. One day, they would leave the protective walls and re-enter the outside world. A few might succeed in their new lives, but most would probably either join a convent to stay within the safety of institutionalization or fall back into a life of abuse and prostitution. It wasn't a death sentence, but a woman who couldn't support herself would always be a step away from the streets.

As I watched the ceiling fan spin overhead, the hypnotic blur of the blades gave focus to my thoughts. That night, I realized that I wanted to help other women achieve financial, political, and sexual freedom so they could live independent, original lives. Even if I hadn't fully achieved it yet myself, I wanted to share the opportunity with others. And I had the means to do it.

I finally fell asleep, but before I knew it, crowing roosters broke my uneasy slumber. It took a minute to adjust to my surroundings. I couldn't remember where I was or how I got there. The lumpy mattress and the mended nightshirt triggered a slow wave of recognition. The Windsor Girls Home. The broken-down taxi. The horseback ride that I never went on.

Fighting my way back toward wakefulness, I thought of something I could do for the girls. I could take them on a special outing—I could take them horseback riding. I rose quietly so I wouldn't wake my sleeping roommates, then dressed and headed for the kitchen. Following the rich smell of Jamaican coffee and of peppers and onions frying on the stove, I found Shamara, cooking breakfast.

"Good morning!" Shamara held out a cup of steaming coffee.

"Thank you! It smells delicious in here," I said. "What are you making?"

"Let's see ... akee, boiled bananas, salt fish, and bammies—round cakes made from cassava flour."

"I can't wait," I said. "Can I help?"

"You just sit there and relax. I have everything under control."

I sipped my coffee in silence for a few minutes, then launched into my pitch. "I've been thinking about what I could do for the girls while I'm here. Something special. I was hoping I could take them on a little adventure today."

Shamara gave me the same suspicious eye she'd flashed when the taxi driver and I first showed up outside the gates. "Like what?"

"I thought about what we discussed yesterday, showing the girls the possibilities in life, and I want to take some of them horseback riding on the beach. Show them a different world than the one they know."

Shamara shook her head and flipped the bammies browning on the stovetop griddle. Already, the kitchen was hot and little drops of sweat had formed on her forehead.

"I don't think so. That's for tourists. And it's expensive. Besides, there are more important things we need. The plumbing is broke in the bathroom, and we need padlocks on the lockers and new paint for the kitchen." She looked at me as if she could go on and on.

"I'll take care of it."

"Take care of what?" A confused look crossed her face, and she cocked her head to one side.

"The plumbing, the padlocks, the paint. All of it. And the horseback riding is on me."

Shamara burst out laughing. "You don't take no for an answer, do you?"

The girls began to shuffle into the cafeteria for breakfast, and I helped Shamara feed all sixty of them. I sat down with a plate of food and devoured the meal with ravenous enthusiasm. My eyes rolled back in my head when I had my first taste of a bammy, the perfect complement to fried fish. The bammy was reminiscent of a tortilla, but with an earthier taste. I was fast becoming a fan of Jamaican food.

After breakfast, Shamara and I went to town to buy the paint and padlocks from the hardware store. She drove an old white van, used as a bus for the girls, but it was in far better condition than the dilapidated taxi that had left me stranded the day before. Since we didn't know exactly what supplies would be needed to repair the plumbing, I left the salesman at the hardware store with a check to cover the estimated expenses.

Back at the Windsor Girls Home, the other workers were beginning to acknowledge that I wasn't just a gawking tourist. When they realized that I truly wanted to help, they warmed up to me—like Shamara had. I stopped in the office and called to make arrangements with the stable. Based on their good behavior, Shamara had chosen eight of the older girls for our little expedition, including the three that I had gotten to know the day before. After I made my call, I went to the kitchen to help prepare lunches for the riders. An hour later, the van from the stable showed up.

"You sure you can manage the rest of the day without me?" Shamara asked the woman who stood by, watching us climb into the van.

"No problem." She was a trim Jamaican, probably about thirty, dressed in a plain white blouse and a simple skirt.

The girls left behind looked at us longingly. They seemed to want to escape the prison, too—if only for a few hours. I knew I could do something to help the girls at Windsor, but I couldn't free them all. Still, I was beginning to be the change I wanted to see in the world.

I had booked a guided horseback ride on the beach. There were four guides for the eight girls, so each rider would get plenty of attention and supervision. At the stable, the girls gathered around me, clutching at my hands and arms. With every snort and whinny of the horses, the skittish girls jumped and flinched.

"You don't need to be afraid," I explained as I patted the neck of a sorrel mare. "The horses may be big, but they are so gentle and sweet, nothing bad will happen." Easy for me to say. I had spent my whole life around horses.

"I've never been on a horse before, Miss Barbara," Monique whispered, her eyes wide with fear. "What if it throws me off?"

"Don't worry," I said. "The guides will take good care of you, and I'll be right here the whole time." I watched as she tentatively stroked her horse's mane while the guide gave her a leg up into the saddle.

Although I'd only met the girls the day before and didn't know them very well, I knew horses. They were loyal, sociable, and eminently capable. A horse would keep a secret, no matter how awful it was. I could only imagine a fraction of what these girls had been through, but by introducing them to horses, I was sharing what I considered to be a little bit of heaven on Earth. On a more tangible level, I thought that if I could help them overcome their fear of horses, perhaps they could overcome other obstacles on their own.

Once we had all mounted up, we rode single file down a path through the trees. The dense forest was cool, even in the heat of the afternoon. Palm fronds rustled in the breeze, and soft ferns uncurled on the damp jungle floor. We passed waterfalls that splashed across the trail, and I watched many of the girls reach out to run their fingers through the gushing water, delighted by the cool splatter against their hands. I encouraged Monique to do the same, and as her hand made contact with the water, she giggled and pulled it back.

"Go ahead, try it again," I said, reining my horse to a stop.

She shot her hand back into the waterfall and let the cool cascade sluice through her fingers. "That feels good," she said, laughing through her missing teeth.

I grinned at her. We caught up with the rest of the group and headed toward the beach. When we arrived, we all dismounted. Several of the girls had flung their shoes into the wet sand as they ran straight for the water, fully clothed, with dreadlocks flying behind them like flags in the wind.

The water slid off their bodies, and their skin glistened in the sun. I was surprised to discover that, even though these girls had been raised on an island, many of them didn't know how to swim. They waded into the surf and splashed each other with the salty froth, playing with the abandon of youth. Some dolphins cruised by, and a few of the swimmers imitated their easy sail through the water. For several hours, the girls bounced about in the water, their cares and worries temporarily forgotten.

I thought of how these free-spirited girls were more appreciative than many women I knew back in the States, who took their blessings for granted yet were trapped by fear and inertia within their own mental prisons. These girls were real victims, and they put things in perspective for me.

Naomi lobbed a clump of white sand at an unsuspecting Marsha, who gave chase. Monique stood nearby, watching the action on the beach with a huge smile on her face. Shading my eyes with my hands, I looked back toward the shore and saw the van from the stable emerge on a gravel road that had been hidden by the trees. Shamara got out and gathered up our lunch supplies. She huffed her way across the sand, juggling her load. When she neared the rest of the group, she propped up a striped umbrella and settled into a beach chair.

I stood next to my horse near one of the guides. He was a Rasta, and he seemed to be enjoying the day.

"They're having so much fun," I said, watching the circus of activities.

"It be very nice. What you're doing for them." His well-worn chaps hung low on his hips, and he held a strand of grass between his teeth.

"They've given me so much more than what I have given them." It sounded corny when I said it out loud, but it was true.

"Ya, but it still be very nice. Maybe I show you something." He started to unbuckle his chaps. "Have you ever flown before?"

"Only on an airplane. What about you?" I couldn't tell if he was flirting with me, stoned out of his mind, or both.

"When Jah is within, all things are possible."

"Show me," I said, accepting the challenge.

The guide shed his chaps and mounted his horse. Following his lead, I put a foot in my stirrup and climbed astride my horse, ready to be enlightened by a Rasta wrangler. With a flick of his reins, the guide let out a shout. "Irie!"

Together, our horses galloped toward the sea. I waited for the guide to change direction, but he headed straight into the surf. As the waves broke around us, the horses surged forward, part running, part swimming, and the Rasta was right. It felt just like flying. For a moment, I was Pegasus.

The girls on the shore shouted and cheered, clamoring to take a turn. I looked to Shamara for approval, and she nodded with a smile. They traveled in pairs, each guide escorting a willing girl into the froth. I could hear shrieks of joy and laughter when their horses took "flight," galloping through the waves.

Not every girl was brave enough to fly. Monique hung back from the others.

"Do you want to try?" I could understand her trepidation.

Monique chewed her bottom lip and looked from me to the other girls and back again. "Yes, ma'am. I want to try, but I'm scared."

I took both of our horses and led them toward the water, tying Monique's horse to a large piece of driftwood on the beach. Eager to experience the rush again, I got on my horse and demonstrated for Monique before I took her into the water.

"It's really quite easy." I dismounted when I returned to shore. "You don't have to do anything except trust your horse."

Emboldened, she came over to the horse. I gave her a leg up, and she hopped astride. Her small hands gripped the reins and clenched the saddle horn. Taking hold of the lead rope tied to her horse's halter, I mounted my own horse, leaving a slack loop between us. I started toward the water and looked back as Monique closed her eyes. Her well-trained mare followed mine out into the water. As we ventured a little deeper, the horses lifted off the ocean floor, buoyed by the salt water.

Monique flicked her eyes open and looked down into the frothy water. "We're flying, Miss Barbara! We're flying!"

She laughed and tentatively lifted one hand off the saddle horn just long enough to wave. I waved back. By the time we returned to shore, I was so hungry my stomach could have eaten itself. I hadn't realized how much energy it took to supervise a group of inexperienced girls, especially those starved for attention.

Shamara had spread out the sandwiches and salads we'd brought along, and we all picnicked on the beach. After lunch, the girls and I built elaborate sandcastles, bolstered by turrets and surrounded by moats. Shamara had the misfortune of falling asleep in the sun, and some of the girls buried her arms in the sand. When she woke, Shamara pretended to be annoyed but couldn't help but laugh. With my permission, Monique used my camera to capture our day on the beach. I knew the girls had Internet access through the school's computer, so I promised to share the photos with them online.

Salty streaks of ocean water dried on the girls' dark skin and turned their arms and legs an ashen gray. On the ride back to Windsor, the girls chattered incessantly about their "magic day." By the time we arrived at the gate, the sun had started its plunge below the horizon and gentle gusts of evening wind moved over the island.

———※———

I didn't stay at the Windsor Girls Home that night. The van from the stable dropped me off at Hedo, where I shed my sandy clothes and collapsed into bed. My body was tucked in for the night, but my mind still rose and fell with the motion of the waves and the weightlessness of the horses. In the low light of my room, I stared up at my reflection in the silly mirror above my bed. In two days, I had discovered treasures that gave me more satisfaction than anything I had ever bought.

I returned to the Windsor Girls Home every day for the rest of my Jamaican stay. My daily visits supplanted my earlier interest in the swingers at Hedo and their alternative lifestyle. Aside from the horseback excursion, we didn't do anything special, but the girls found a sudden passion for doing homework and chores—as long as I was there with them. I taught classes, cooked lunches, and sewed—ordinary tasks with extraordinary rewards. The girls had an endless supply of love to give, and I tried to return as much as I got.

The day before I planned to leave Jamaica, Shamara and I were in the kitchen, washing the lunch dishes. Much as I was ready to get back to my life, I was sad to be leaving.

"I feel like I've discovered something valuable here, Shamara, and I don't want to let it go."

In Jamaica, the standard of living was low, yet the payoff for embracing the lifestyle was huge. The people had fewer possessions than folks in the States, yet they seemed more joyful. Despite having very little money, most of them were lighthearted and passionate. Their world revolved around music, dance, and food. That was the life for me!

Then there were the girls. I didn't know how I was going to say good-bye to my protégé photographer, Monique. I wondered if skinny little Marsha would ever fill out and if Naomi would ever tend children of her own instead of just chickens.

"You've been deep in thought all day," Shamara commented, as she put away the last pot and hung up her dishtowel. The tiny kitchen was spotless, carefully maintained by Shamara's sense of pride. There were no granite countertops or butcher-block islands, but everything in that kitchen had its place. I had been comfortable in the homey space from the first day I helped prepare lunch.

I sighed with a tired shrug and plopped down on a kitchen chair. "I'm going to miss you and the girls so much. I can't stop thinking about it."

Shamara poured two glasses of limeade and joined me at the table. We drank in silence before she finally spoke. "You know what I think?"

"What's that?"

"I think you came here for a reason," Shamara said. "Maybe you were sent by Jah, but you helped the girls see things differently. You were brought here to point them toward a different destiny."

"I'm only visiting. You're making a difference every day." The leaky faucet dripped into the kitchen sink, as if it were begging me to stay. How could I leave when the plumbing still needed work?

Shamara held up her index finger. "You've shown these girls a whole new side of life. I couldn't do that. You sparked their curiosity about the world. There are no accidents, Barbara. It was fate that brought you here."

Maybe she was right. Maybe my life had taken the twists and turns it had so that I could go to an island in the middle of the Caribbean and give a little girl hope. During the week I spent at Windsor, I had worked with many young women. I didn't know for sure if I had made a difference, but if I changed the life of just one girl, it was worth it. I knew that when I left Jamaica, I would be a different person than I was when I arrived.

—⁂—

On my last day at the Windsor Girls Home, the girls invited me to stay for a special dinner. Instead of eating in the covered cafeteria, they transformed a section of the open balcony into a dining room. Fat, white candles lined the railing. Their flames flickered in the night. A yellowed lace runner stretched the length of the shaky wooden table, and mismatched silverware rested on faded green napkins. The table was laden with a bounty of food.

I recalled my first meal at Windsor, when every flavor was new and every dish was an experiment. The exotic seasonings had captured my soul and transformed my taste buds into an international palate. Even before I left, I craved Jamaican food and started to wonder how I could replicate it at home.

Flattered by the efforts of the girls on my behalf, I piled my plate high with curry goat stew, fried plantain, sweet cabbage, and beef patties. After taking my plate to an empty spot at the table, I returned to the spread and ladled out a big bowl of pepper-pot soup. I ate until I thought I would burst.

"Miss Barbara," Marsha said. "Don't you forget dessert. We made you a rum cake."

Shamara cleared her throat. The girls got up from the table and assembled along the balcony. I immediately spotted the ones I knew best, but all the faces were familiar to me by then.

"What's this?" I asked, suddenly self-conscious about being the guest of honor.

Monique pointed at me. "This for you, Miss Barbara."

The girls began to hum, and they swayed their bodies in unison. With clear, strong voices, they started to sing, and I realized it was the Bob Marley song, "One Love." It wasn't the song that pushed me over the edge. It was the precious way they had put it together and the way they sang their hearts out. For me. They sang a cappella, and it was the most beautiful song I had ever heard.

I cried. I cried like a little girl. And I cried like a mother, knowing that I was probably never going to see these children again. I knew that when I left, lessons would still need to be taught, clothes would still need to be mended, meals would still need to be cooked, and through it all, the wolves would still be waiting at the door for a moment of weakness.

When I finished bawling, I started to sing along, and soon our party spilled out onto the grass below. Someone turned on a radio, and we switched over to the current pop songs that teenage girls enjoyed the world over. We laughed and danced, blissfully ignorant of the walls that fenced us in.

We partied until my taxi came and the driver sounded his horn at the gate. I gathered up the girls to say good-bye. I would miss Naomi's fierce fidelity to her friends, Marsha's uninhibited dance moves, and Monique's courage to try new things when every chance she'd ever taken had gone disastrously wrong. As I hugged every last girl, they cried and whimpered, begging me not to go.

I found Shamara and thanked her wholeheartedly. She wrapped her arms around me and pulled me close.

"Thank you, Barbara."

"You are most welcome," I said. "You have no idea what my time here has meant to me. I have a wonderful family back home, but you and the girls—you are family, too."

We promised to stay in touch, and my tears started again. They didn't stop until the taxi had taken me down the hill and back to the resort. But unlike other times when I felt sad or upset, I didn't feel empty or ashamed. Rather, I felt the fullness of the incredible way that we'd been able to share our worlds with one another. I was lucky to have known them.

I thought about how I had cursed about my lost baggage when I had first arrived in Ireland. Looking back, it was trivial and unimportant, a minor nuisance, but at the time, it felt like an ordeal. These girls were trapped behind a fence and would be raped if they ventured outside the gates. *That* was an ordeal, and some had been through much worse. I didn't want to take my freedom for granted. Helping others gave me a tremendous sense of satisfaction, and I realized that when I was giving, I felt most alive.

Still, I couldn't get that final scene out of my head. In the darkness, someone had closed the heavy gate. I heard the clank of the chain being looped through the fence and the snap of the padlock securing the premises. Highlighted from behind by the last of the evening's candles, the girls stood clinging to the fence. I couldn't see their faces, but their silhouettes burned into my heart.

Chapter 19

COMING HOME

When I returned home from Jamaica in the fall, the island felt worlds away. It seemed less real, more dreamlike, but there was no denying its effect on me. Even though I launched with hopes of a hedonistic experience, I found more pleasure in activities that fulfilled my soul—teaching, sharing, giving.

The following year, I left Riverside and moved into a townhouse in San Diego, just a few blocks from the beach. My daughters came to visit for the holidays, and while it seemed at first like starting over, it definitely felt like home. The three of us walked on the beach, baked Christmas cookies, and sipped hot cocoa in front of the fireplace, pretending it was cold outside. We wrapped presents and decorated the tree. With each ornament I hung, I spoke a few words about something I loved. I voiced a chant, a mantra, and opened up my soul to my daughters.

"I love to love because I need to be loved. I love my friends and family because I need that human connection. I love to give because I get so much back. I love sex—I'm not going to explain that one." We all laughed. "I love to laugh, and sometimes cry. I love my anger because it motivates me to change. I love my fear; it challenges me. I love my courage because it makes me take risks to conquer my fear."

"Mom, I want to be more like you," Molly said. "I don't want to let fear stop me from taking risks."

"I agree," said Kelly. "And I can't wait to ride horses with you in Ireland."

Somewhere along my journey, I had grown into a woman who wanted to understand her daughters instead of one who needed to be understood and forgiven by them. "Perfect" was no longer a realistic expectation for any of us, but my daughters and I had settled into a more honest relationship. Together, we talked without pretense about the daily struggles that we faced in our lives. We openly broached subjects that were off-limits with my own mother—conflict, authenticity, and even sex. I knew that our individual religious and political views would change as each of us grew and learned more about life, but my heart gladdened whenever we entered an intelligent, unbiased discussion.

As an unintended consequence of my divorce, my daughters established a closer relationship with each other. We had moved beyond the familial hierarchy of mother and daughter and into the realm of friends. I knew I had a role in shaping my fiercely independent daughters into the strong yet compassionate women they had become, and I continued to support them and offer opportunities whenever I could. But in the end, each one would have to decide what was best for her. Each of them would have to take the first and hardest step—figuring out who she was. Only then could she determine what she wanted.

Kelly was starting college and thinking of studying journalism, and Molly was beginning graduate school, looking forward to a career in marketing. I recognized that at this stage of their lives, I wasn't needed as much, just like Grandma Pat had said all those years before. I found a way to nurture other girls and women by starting a foundation to facilitate programs that help women realize their dreams of achieving a full and successful life. Although I still craved adventure and travel, I wanted to bring insight and opportunity to women in my new hometown.

My time in Jamaica had made me realize how fortunate I was to have caring parents. There were times when I felt alone, but I was not an orphan. Whenever my fear, laziness, and self-doubt kept me from being all I could be, I reminded myself that my jail was only in my mind. And I held the key to my freedom. Girls like Monique, Marsha, and Naomi would never have the kind of opportunities that I didn't think twice about. I knew there were other girls in similar circumstances all around the world, and this knowledge reinforced my commitment to treasure all that I had and not take anything for granted.

With my divorce, I rebelled against my parents' values, and when their own marriage failed, I called them out as hypocrites to anyone who would listen. But my parents did the best they could with the tools they had. I was beginning to understand this and to forgive them for things I had held against them for many years. As I started this transition, I felt the reward of letting go. It was time to make amends.

Impulsively, I hopped in my car on New Year's Day and drove north to Carlsbad, where both my parents still resided. Well into their seventies, each of them had a live-in lover. I had to give them credit for being bold enough to cast aside what other people might think about that. Nearing my mother's neighborhood, I saw it through the eyes of poor Jamaican girls who had grown up in tin–and–tar paper shacks. As I drove up, I spotted my mother gardening in her yard.

"Hi, Mom," I said, letting myself through the gate. "You busy?"

"Oh, hello, Barb. Just catching up on some yard work." She wasn't surprised by my unannounced arrival, or if she was, she hid it well.

The year-round flowerbeds were already immaculate, but my mother pulled tiny weeds from the soil and trimmed away blossoms that were one day past their peak. She still focused on appearances. When I offered to help, she insisted on putting her things away and making some tea. We went inside, and I sat on the same sofa my parents had shared when they were married. Mom made small talk while she set the kettle to boil, and I played along, waiting for the right opportunity to bare my soul. I felt vulnerable, but daring. Ready to let go of past resentments and move into the future.

"Remember when I went to Jamaica?" I asked, accepting the cup of tea that my mother offered. I had been back for over a year, and my mother had never asked about my trip.

"Oh, yes. Did you have a good time?"

I sipped tea from the china cup and told her about my trip. The resort, the home, the scuba diving—I didn't leave anything out. Well, except maybe the part about smoking pot. That would have been a little much. While most of my friends just wanted to hear about the nude beaches and wild parties at the resort, my mother showed genuine interest in my experiences at the Windsor Girls Home. She was moved by the plight of the girls and angered by the men who preyed on them. I told her how I'd since helped one of the Jamaican girls start a small chicken farm so she could leave Windsor and find her own path to independence.

It felt like we'd turned the clock back to when I returned home from a church trip to Mexico, where I'd done relief work. Or maybe even back to my internship in the Canary Islands when I discovered that physical therapy wasn't just a career for me, but a calling. After I returned from those missions, my mother listened patiently while I told her every last detail about the things I'd seen and the people I'd helped. When I was through, she told me she was proud of me.

Back then, I felt as if anything were possible, as if I could solve all the world's problems, and a big part of my self-assured attitude came from my mother's belief in me. As I grew older and realized how different my values were from those taught by the church of my youth, I found it hard to maintain that inner confidence. I lost even more self-esteem while married to Jay when I lived as who I was supposed to be instead of who I really was. But after moving forward on my own, I had regained my confidence. I no longer gave in to my fears; instead, I found the courage to overcome them.

"I know I haven't always shown it," I began, "but I want you to know how much I appreciate everything you've done for me over the years."

My mother set down her tea and looked at me skeptically, as if I were pulling some kind of trick.

"When I think of all the opportunities you have given me, opportunities those girls in Jamaica will never have ..." I started to tear up.

"It's just what mothers do," she said, patting my hand. "You know how it is. You do the same for your girls."

"They're away at school. They don't need me anymore." A tear rolled down my cheek, and I wiped it away with my free hand.

"That's not true. They need you now more than ever."

Here goes, I thought. My mother was about to say something about me "gallivanting all over the world" when I had responsibilities at home. But the lecture never came. She just squeezed my hand. When she let go, her hand went to her throat in a nervous flutter.

"When your father and I decided to go our separate ways," she said with some difficulty, "I thought you'd be the first to say, 'I told you so.'"

"I might not have said it, but I thought it more than once," I confessed. I rubbed my palms along the lengths of my thighs, reflecting uncomfortably on those tense and frustrating times.

"After all the things I said to you while you were going through your divorce—even after it was final—I don't blame you."

Was that an apology? Maybe not to the casual observer, but opening the door to the possibility that she might have been wrong was as close as my mother ever got to saying she was sorry. I accepted the words, grateful for her response.

She gave me a stilted hug, then stood and went to the kitchen. When she returned with the teapot, she refilled our cups. Ever the proper hostess.

"How are you handling things on your own?" I asked. "Are you okay? Really? Do you know I love you?" She had never asked me those questions when Jay and I split up, and I wished she had. Dealing with the dark side of relationships was painful. Oftentimes, uncomfortable situations got shelved, and that's why people got blindsided. My mom and I had both learned that the hard way.

"I'm fine. Of course, it's a little hard when your life is uprooted after fifty years, but I'm moving on." She paused. "I'm in a great relationship now. I don't want to talk about the past. I sail on the surface; you're the diver."

True. I realized that it was painful for my mother to admit that she had wasted all those years in a failed marriage. Thankfully, I had set myself free and accepted the risks of living an authentic life while I was still young. My mother had taught me that perceptions matter, but I was learning not to focus on them at the expense of the substance in my life.

"I'm really happy for you, Mom. We are two different people, yet we have many similarities. I'm ready to accept you for who you are and enjoy the things we have in common."

My mother smiled. "So where is your next big adventure taking you, Barb?"

"Nowhere. I'm staying put for a while." I brought my tea to my lips, but it was too hot to drink.

"I'm sure your girls will be happy to hear that."

"I'm taking dance lessons, Mom." I glanced over at her, then down into the shallow bowl of my teacup.

"Oh? What kind?" she asked. Even before I looked up, I knew she had raised her eyebrows.

"Ballroom ... and burlesque." It felt more like a confession than a simple statement.

"Oh, Barbara," my mother said, with something like laughter. "You always do things your own way!"

And that was it. I breathed a deep sigh of relief and let out almost fifty years of trying to be someone other than me. I didn't have to strive to be more like Grandma Pat or struggle against being too much like my mom. I could just be myself—let Barbara be Barbara. Why had it taken me so long to figure that out? I had traveled around the world, searching out all the hidden dimensions of myself, and just when I thought I had most of the answers, I came home to realize that what I wanted most was just to be accepted for who I was. I had to love myself, first. All along, I had looked for love in the wrong places, seeking approval from others. What I really needed was to feel good about myself.

It had to start with me.

Chapter 20

MISS BEHAVING

Back to the Grind was a rustic downtown dive with dim lighting, rough-hewn wood floors, and red velvet sofas. At night, the café's stage and theater space featured live music, and in the rooms above the stage, private instructors gave dance lessons. Kitten deVille held court there. She taught jazz and tap, but her true calling was burlesque. She danced as a featured performer all over Southern California and beyond.

I showed up for my first burlesque lesson not knowing what to expect. Even though I had pulled my hair into a sloppy ponytail, I painted my lips a glossy red and wore sexy lace lingerie beneath my frumpy sweats. There were about twenty of us in the class—an odd assortment of students, homemakers, executives, and retirees. Some looked like dancers, but wrinkles and fat were definitely part of the mix.

Kitten strutted to the center of the room holding a long wooden cane in one hand. Three dancers stood behind her. Bleached blond hair fell around her porcelain face in the bobbed style of a pinup girl from the forties. Her lean body was clad in a long-sleeved black leotard, sheer black leggings, and fluorescent green patent-leather heels. She cracked the cane against the floor, and we all stood at attention.

"Ladies, me and my gals are gonna teach you the finer points of the art of the tease. Are you ready?" She flung her cane to a corner of the room. One of the dance instructors started up the music, and the sound of a slow, trumpet-driven instrumental piece filled the room.

"All right, ladies," Kitten called out. "Let's heat up those bodies."

She started us out with a short warm-up of stretching and bending, typical of any aerobics class. Then the real work started. We learned how to roll our hips in a slow and sensual movement. What at first felt awkward to me soon became fluid and rhythmic, a bit like dancing in Jamaica. We began to learn the art of the strut and practiced cross-steps, shimmies, and booty shakes. Nervous laughter gave way to loud hoots and cheering as we started to get in the groove.

At the end of the first class, I retreated to a corner where I took off my cross-trainers and began to rub my throbbing feet. Kitten sauntered over in her five-inch spikes and gave me some advice.

"Good job, sugar. Next time—less clothes, more heels." She winked as she walked away.

The classes at Back to the Grind were full of giggles and shimmies. I felt an instant connection with all the women there, no matter what their age, weight, or profession. During our practice sessions, I was often sandwiched in between a grandmother (who chose the stage name Dolly Dagger) and a gangly bank executive, or a single mom and a college coed, but in the sisterhood of burlesque, I felt completely at ease. The spirit of Grandma Pat gave me inspiration when the workouts got too intense. She would have absolutely loved it.

Burlesque was all about sensual beauty and feminine mystique. There was something empowering about being a seductress on the stage. For as long as the music played, I lived in a fantasy world where I felt desirable to all, yet completely off-limits. Even though we all took the same lessons, each woman designed a costume and routine to reflect her individual style and chose a unique stage name. I dubbed myself

"Miss Behaving." The bulk of a burlesque performance was the tease, but it built toward something—the big reveal—that kept the audience on the edge.

The burlesque classes evolved into a sort of postmodern quilting bee. Over sparkling wine, I connected with Ruby Champagne, the banker who was roughly my age. We designed glamorous getups that made us feel sophisticated, like old-time movie stars, by gluing sequins on our pasties and creating beautiful beaded panties and satin corsets. Sometimes I danced for Cupcakes Delicious, the college coed, who gave me pointers on how to strut my stuff and let go of my inhibitions. It seemed funny to take advice from a girl young enough to be my daughter, but I was over that. I was willing to learn from anyone who could teach me. Initially, I pretended that my sequined underwear was a two-piece bathing suit as I seductively abandoned the parts of my costume that covered it. I suppose it was liberating to experience that new side of my femininity, but mostly it was exhilarating.

After two months of weekly classes, Kitten announced that the moment we had all been preparing for had arrived. It was time for us to perform. Our class size had dropped from its original enrollment, so I suggested we put on a midsize show at the local hospital where I worked as a volunteer. Everyone loved the idea, especially Kitten.

"You get us in," she said, "and I'll take it from there."

———❦———

"Excuse me, ma'am," the program director drawled over the telephone. He paused for a moment and then asked, "You say you want to come here and do what kind of dance?"

"Burlesque," I replied. "It's dance, theater, and striptease all rolled into one."

"Did you say 'striptease'? As in take off all your clothes and dance around naked?"

"Well, not all of our clothes, but something like that, yes."

The program director laughed. "Oh, no, ma'am. We can't allow that. We try to keep our entertainment clean. Our shows typically involve kids, retirees, and church groups."

It wasn't a convalescent home we were talking about, but a naval hospital brimming with young men and women who had put their lives on the line for our country. They deserved real entertainment, and I said as much to the program director.

"Well, ma'am, we have to consider what the community might say about something like that."

"My grandmother used to dance in USO shows when she was a young woman," I protested.

"I'm pretty sure your grandmother kept her clothes on."

Obviously, he didn't know Grandma Pat.

I switched the phone to my other ear and explained that our dance group met in the theater space of a coffee shop—not some seedy strip club—and consisted of women of all ages, from young military wives to soccer moms to grandmothers. I decided it would probably be best if I didn't mention our seasoned instructor, Kitten de Ville. Instead, I described our intention of putting on a Christmas show to boost morale for those who couldn't be home for the holidays.

The program director began to come around. "I don't know ..."

"What if we promise not to take off all our clothes or show any cleavage?"

"Ma'am, so long as you dance in what you came in, we have a deal."

Once I got the go-ahead from the base, Kitten made most of the arrangements. We carefully planned a G-rated performance with a catered dinner and dancing for all.

On the night of the event, we gathered at the hospital's recreation center. An emcee hosted the show, a professional DJ mixed the dance tunes, and ten professional ballroom dancers—some of whom had been coaches on *Dancing With the Stars*—were brought in to perform. But the burlesque show was definitely the highlight of the night.

Backstage, we did our best to pump each other up.

"Make 'em want you, girl!" urged Ruby, her banker's professionalism locked away for the night.

"Show your sexy!" said Dolly, passing around sparkling gold eye shadow, scattering it like fairy dust. We were ready. Among us, there were eight women, twenty-four costumes, and enough raging eroticism to ignite a forest fire. Pure smoldering heat. That's what I kept saying to myself.

Kitten burst into the room, waving the list in her hand. "Come on, ladies! Let's do this! Put on your eyelashes, apply that last bit of glitter. Watch it, Roxy, your left breast is getting away from you."

Roxy was on the verge of a wardrobe malfunction. She tucked and pulled, but her outfit was losing the battle against gravity. So much skin, so little fabric—a burlesque dancer's biggest nightmare.

Cinnamon Britches was calm before the show, methodically applying her makeup like a soldier preparing for battle. Her costume was barely there, mere wisps of glittery fabric decorating the smooth skin between her tattoos.

As for me, I wore leather chaps and a sequined vest. Fine fishnet covered the rest of my body, allowing my skin to show through and breathe. I adjusted my cowboy hat, canting it at a sassy angle. I knew the audience would never see the sequin-covered satin that masked my breasts and bikini area, but I wore it anyway. It made me feel sexy. I was ready to dance when the backstage light flickered red.

"Show time, girls," Kitten shouted.

The lights went up, and the curtain followed. We stepped out as the trombones revved up—buxom young babes, frail grandmothers, and ordinary middle-aged women. And we were all beautiful.

The music ranged from old-time classics to current pop hits. Each woman had her moment in the spotlight. No matter who was up, or what the song, each performance felt magical. The audience stomped and clapped. Then it was my turn.

The air felt electric, and so did the beat. The jitters that I thought I might get never transpired. I closed my eyes and sank into the rhythm of "Danger Zone." The song consumed me; my body sang the lyrics. With every spin, every twirl, every pause, I fell deeper into the dance. The music pulsed through my body, and I raised my arms slowly as I undulated to the beat, sensuality oozing from every pore. The crowd shouted and applauded their approval.

I peeled away the layers of my masks, one by one, and found myself transported. I was cantering on my horse in Ireland, wind blowing in my hair, rain hitting my face. The beat built, and in my mind, the canter became a gallop. Charging into the surf on my flying steed in Jamaica, I felt free. I lifted my arms to the ceiling and whirled. For one brief moment, I was sure I saw Grandma Pat beside me, dancing and laughing.

I was a chorus girl that night.

I was free.

I was me.

EPILOGUE

For years, I wanted others to change, and I wanted them to give me permission to be who I was … to validate the choices I'd made for myself. Until I learned not to blindly follow a script that others had written, I didn't realize that this permission had to come solely from me.

Finding myself and allowing myself to be that person didn't happen overnight, and I made plenty of mistakes along the way. I have a few regrets, but now I focus on the present and look forward to the future. When the music plays, I dance; when the horse within wants to gallop, I work with her, not against. My journey has taught me the joys of experiencing, learning, and loving, as well as the joy of freedom. And freedom has taught me that taking responsibility brings more joy—the joy of giving and the joy of leading a purposeful life.

To help other women live all their dimensions, I established Mother, Lover, Fighter, Sage—a foundation dedicated to offering workshops, seminars, and scholarships that enhance the lives of women. Proceeds from this book go to my foundation, funding speakers and events to help women access their personal strengths and potential.

Each of us can make a difference.